I0494650

Mindless Stress Therapy

Adult Coloring Book

Volume 1

CVJ Publishing

Copyright

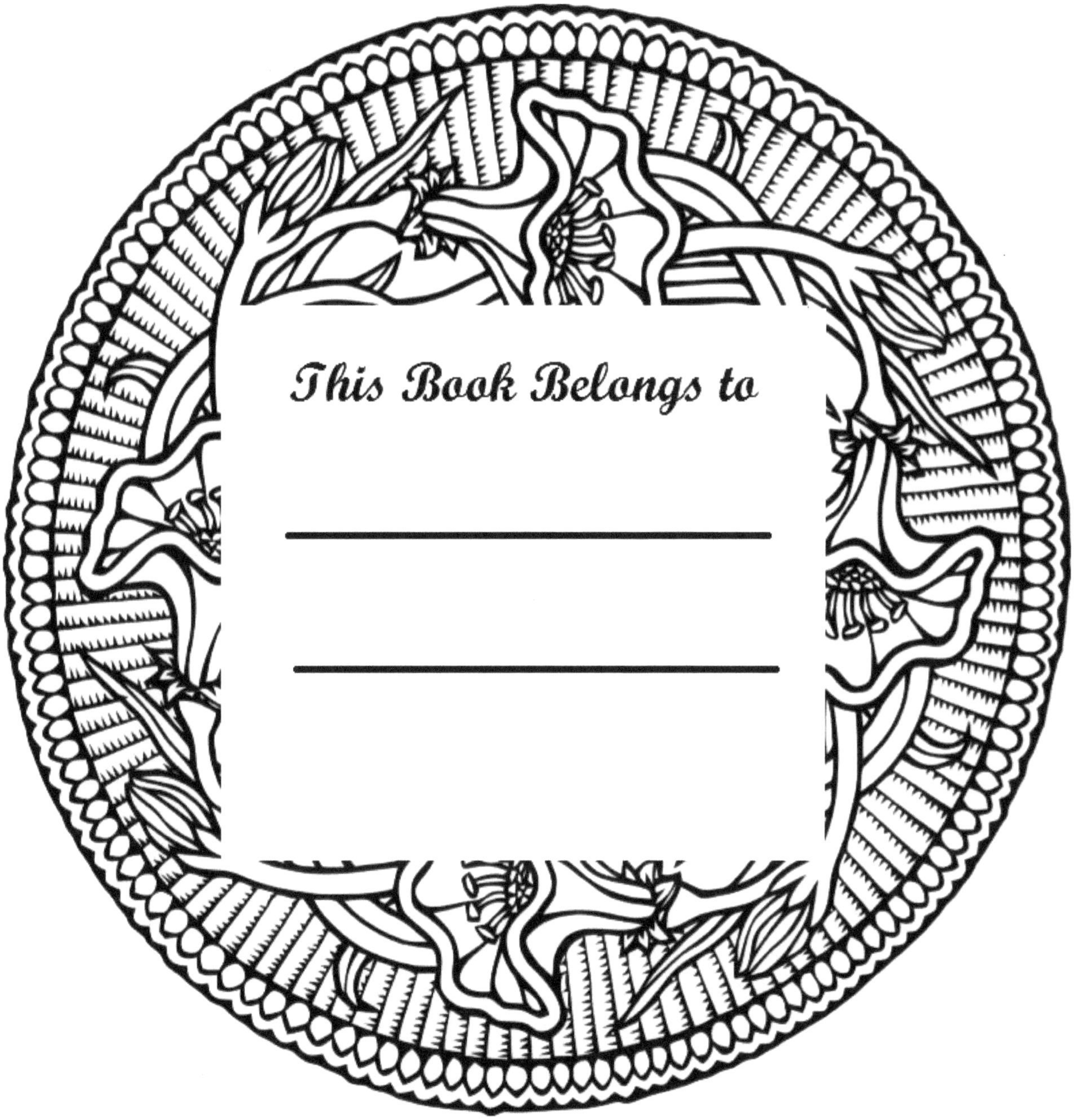
This Book Belongs to
____
____

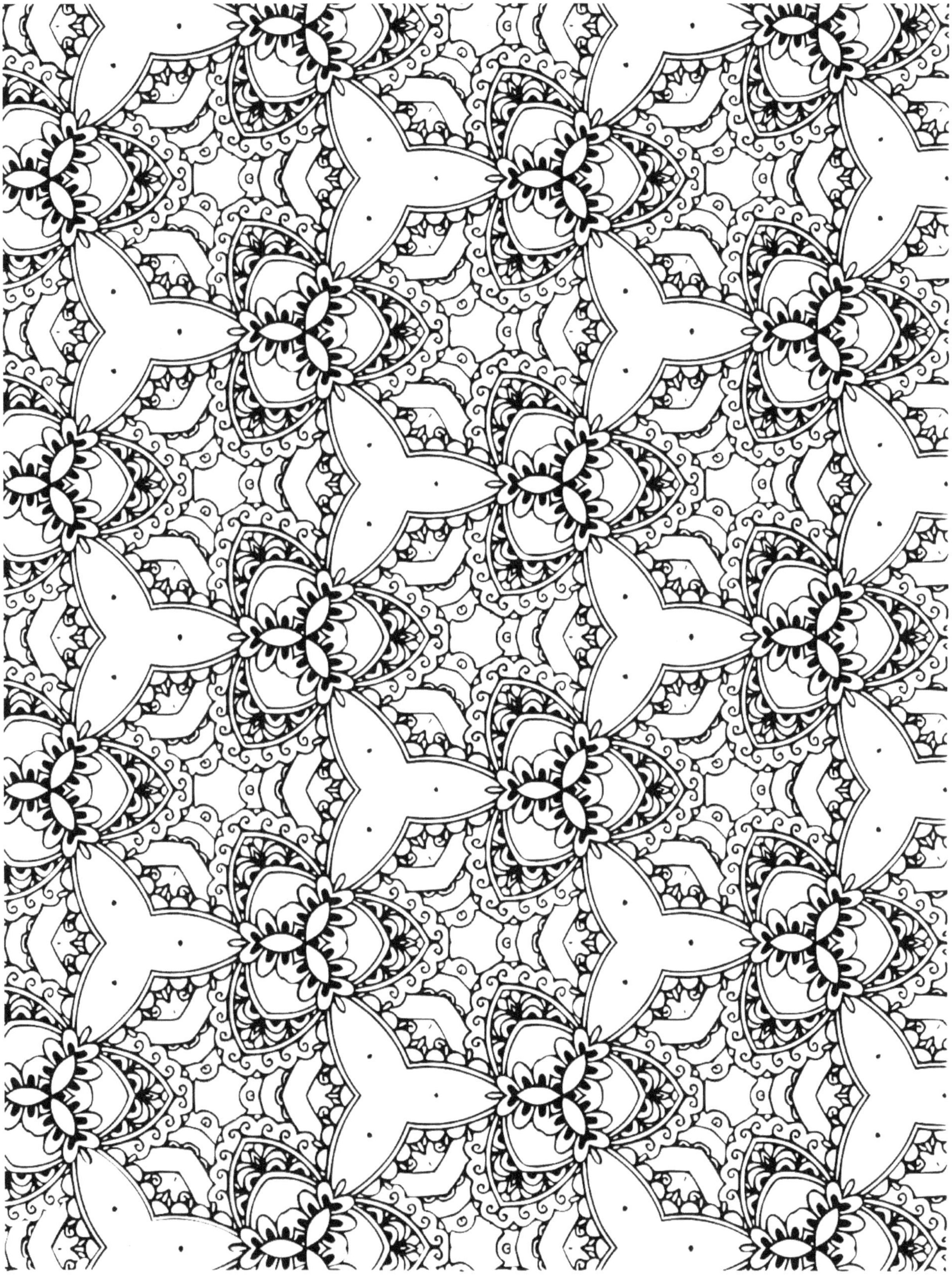

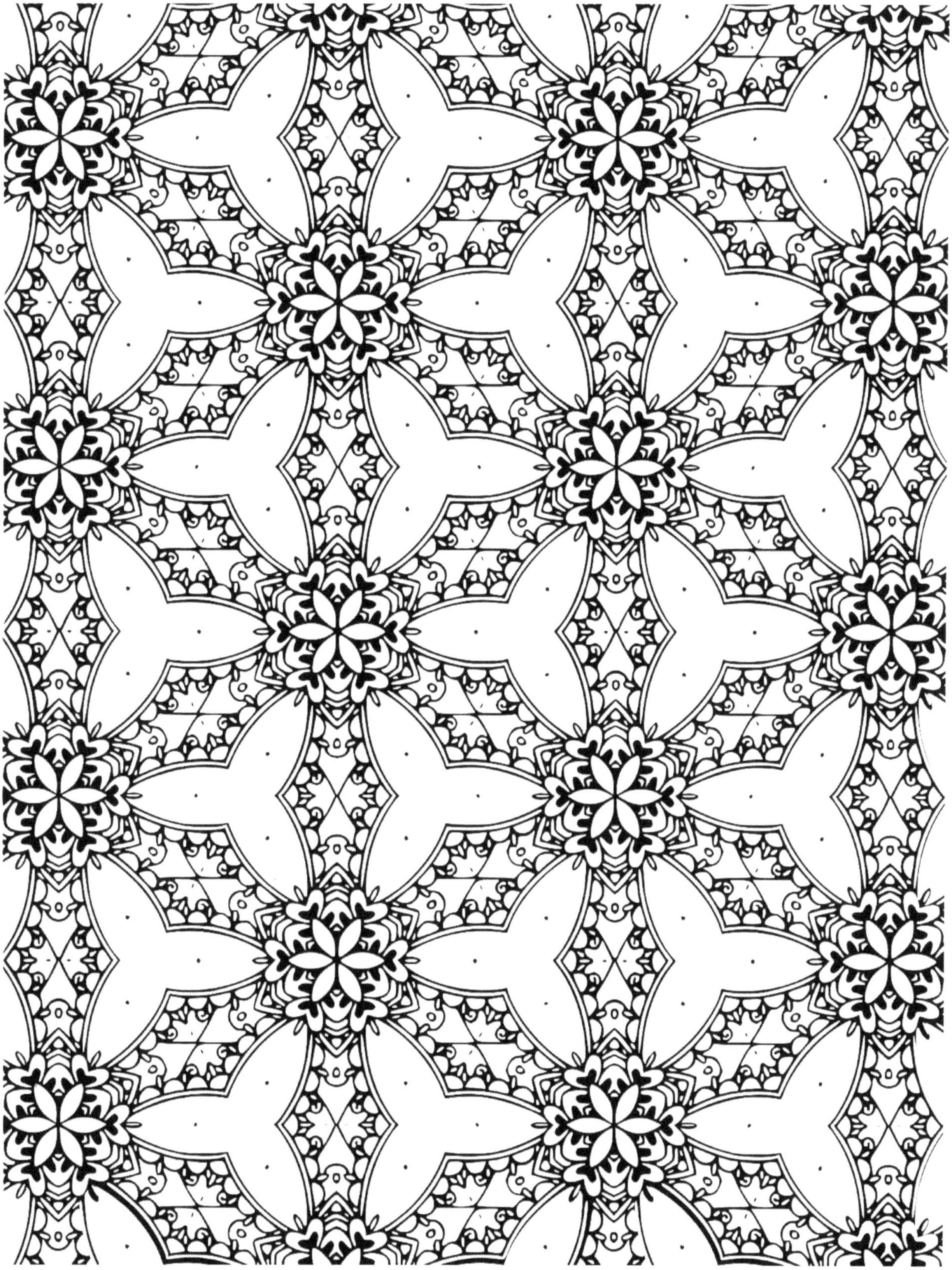

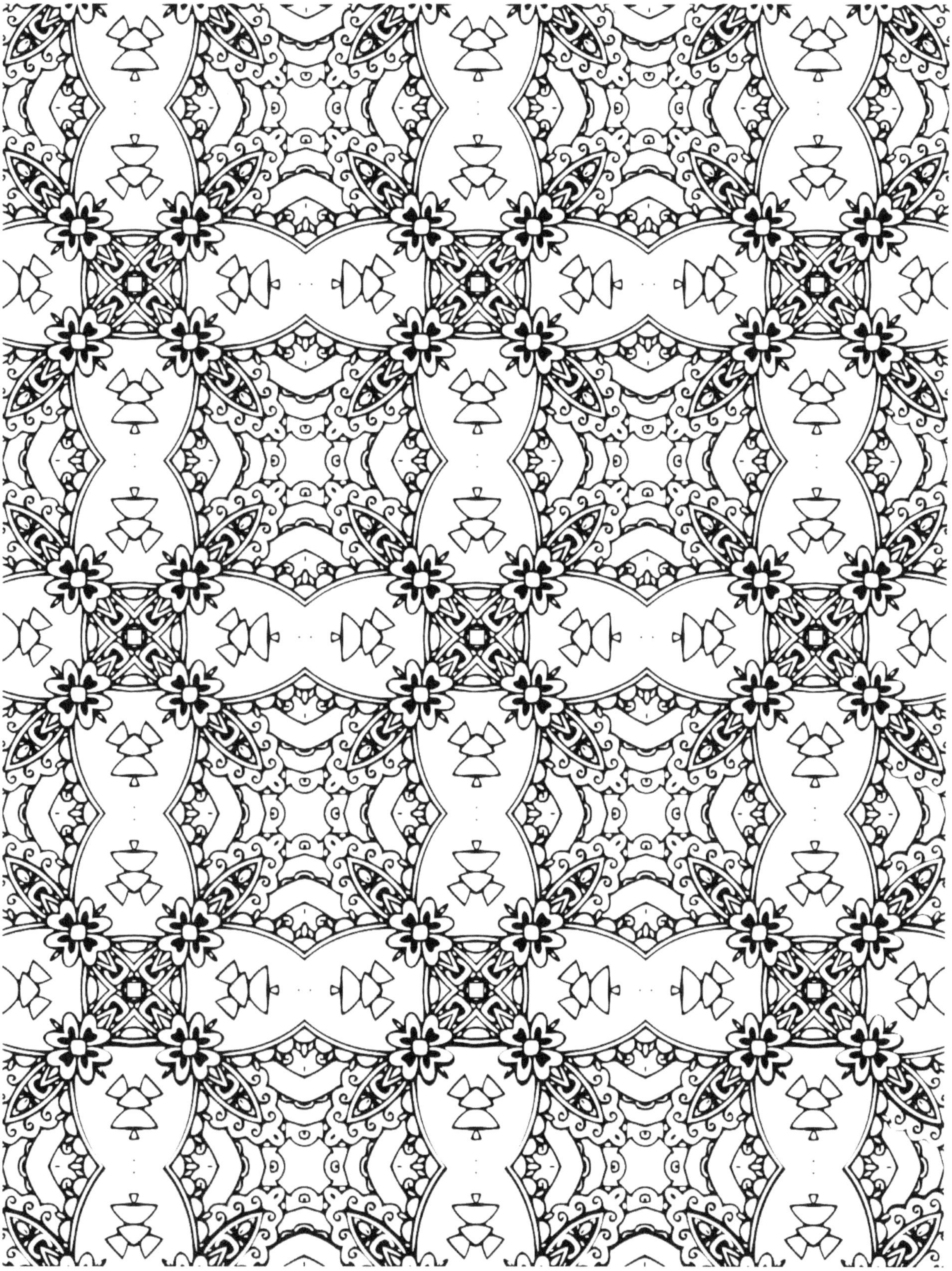

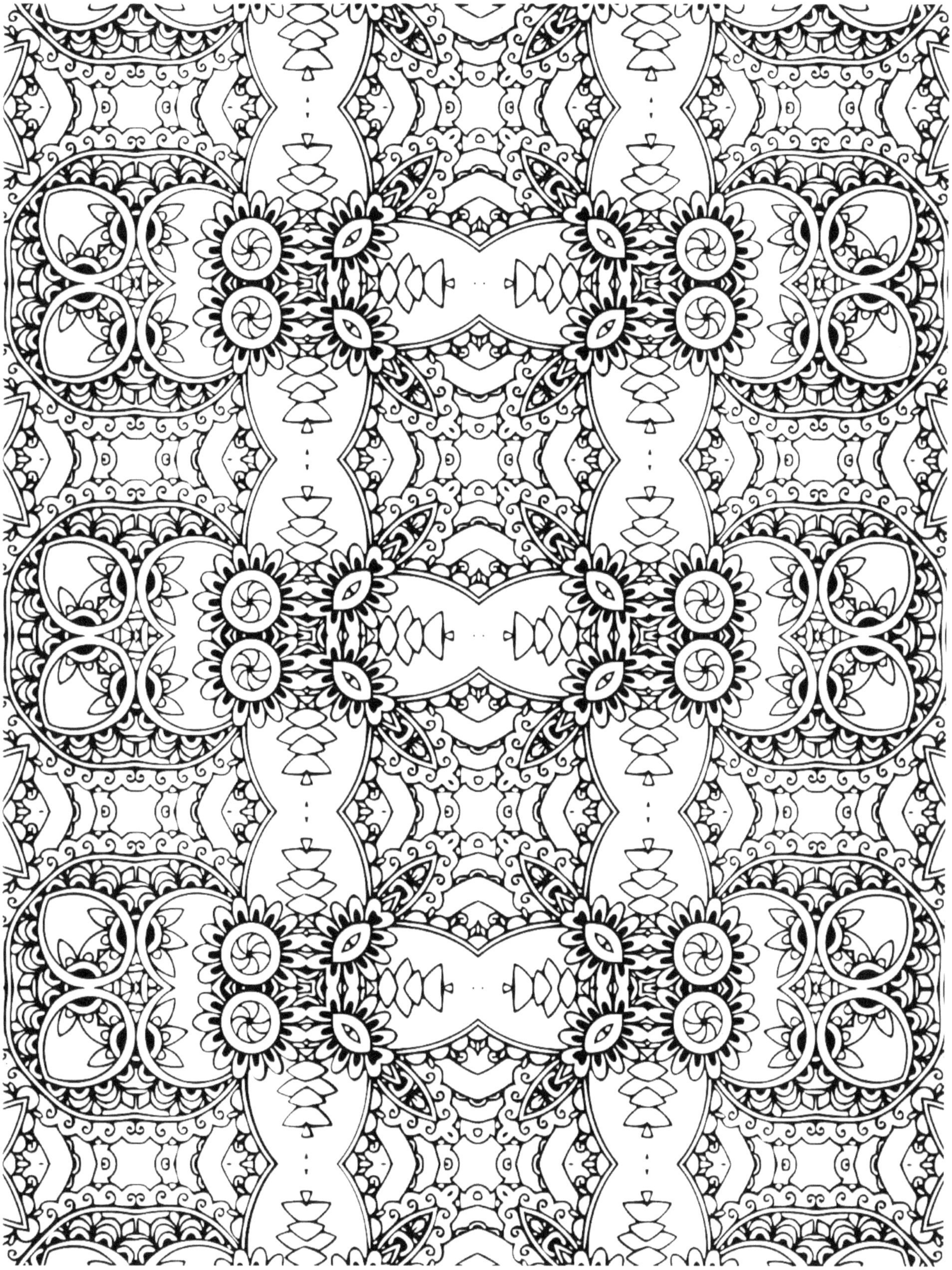

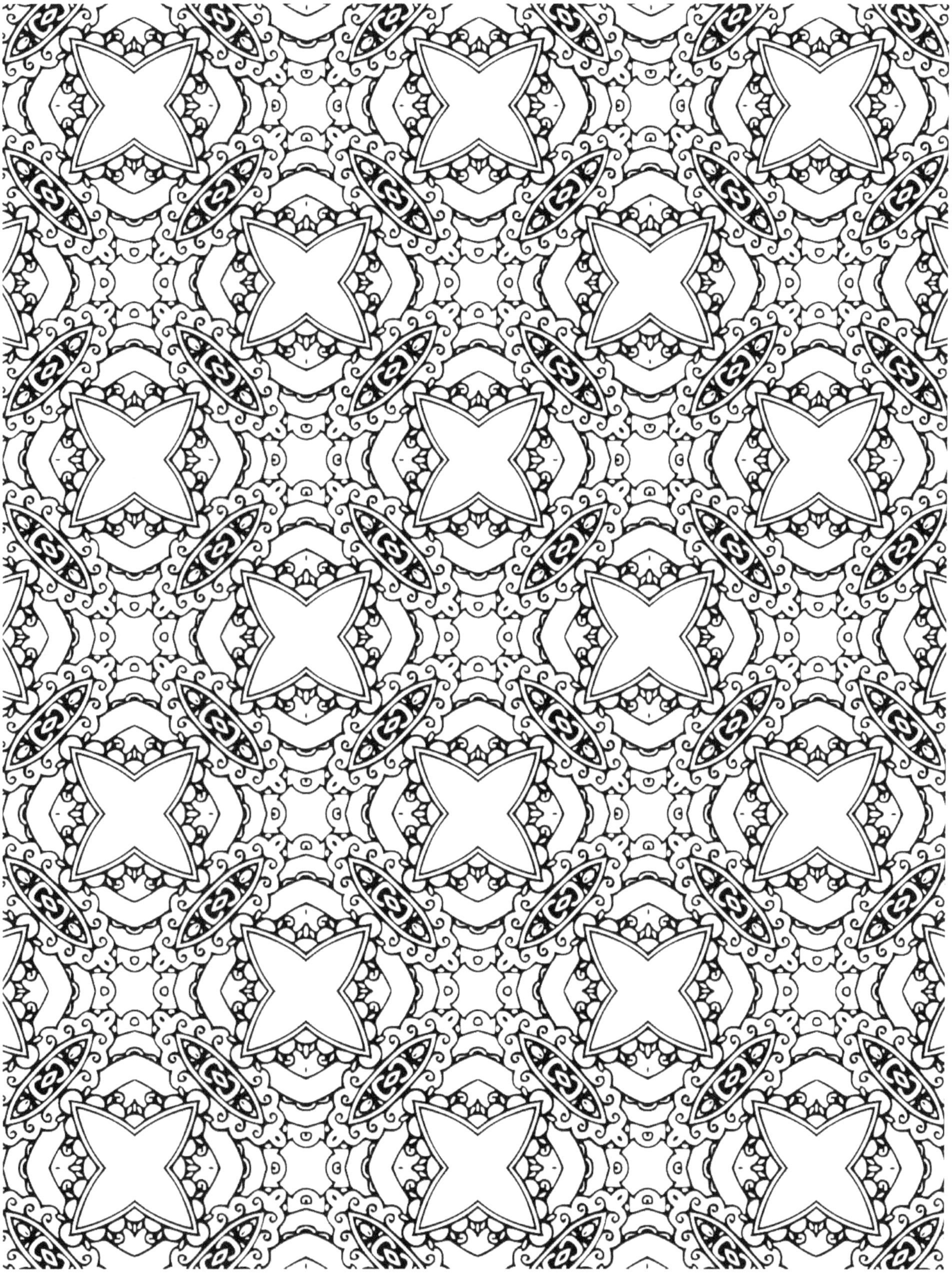

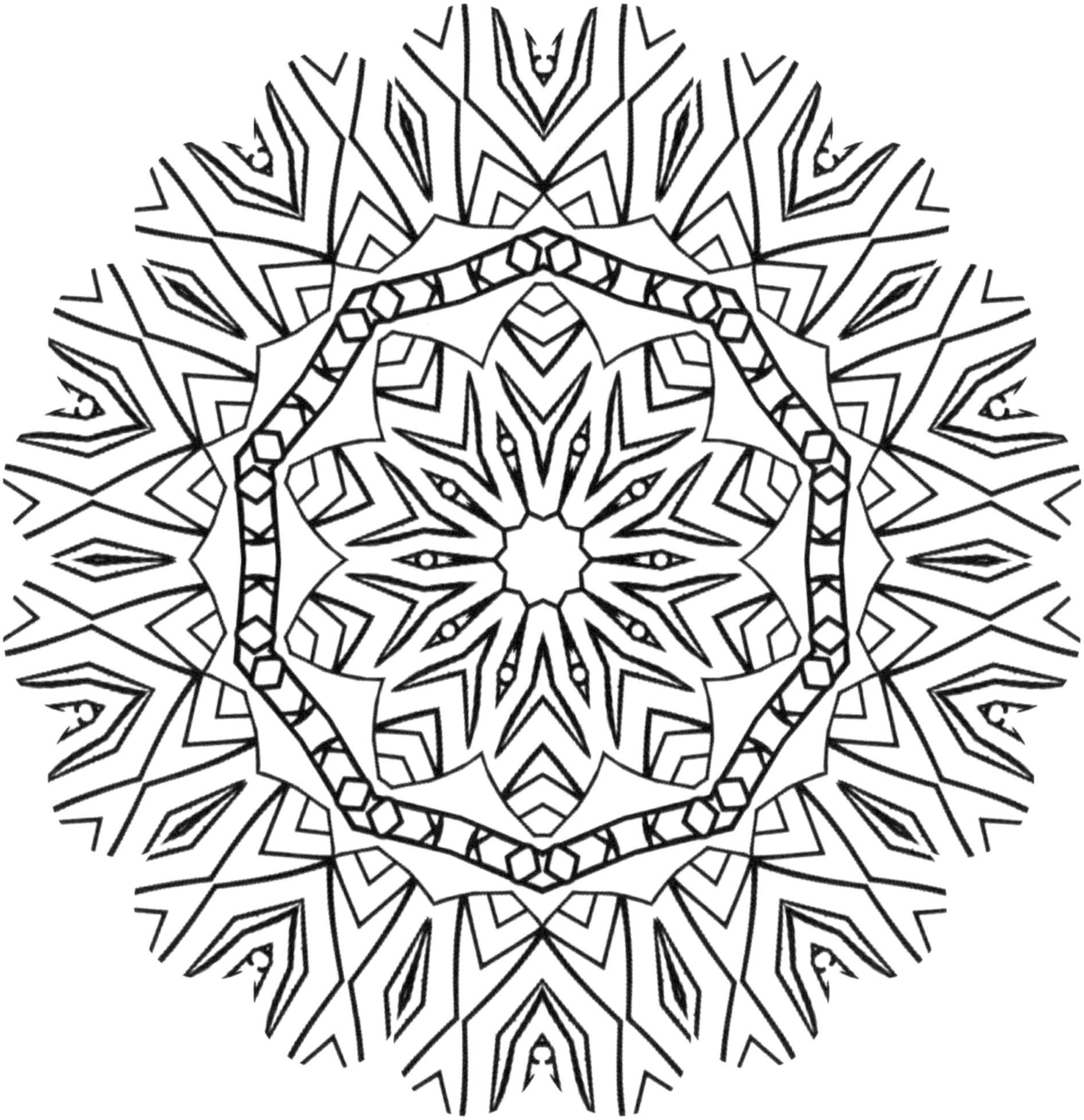

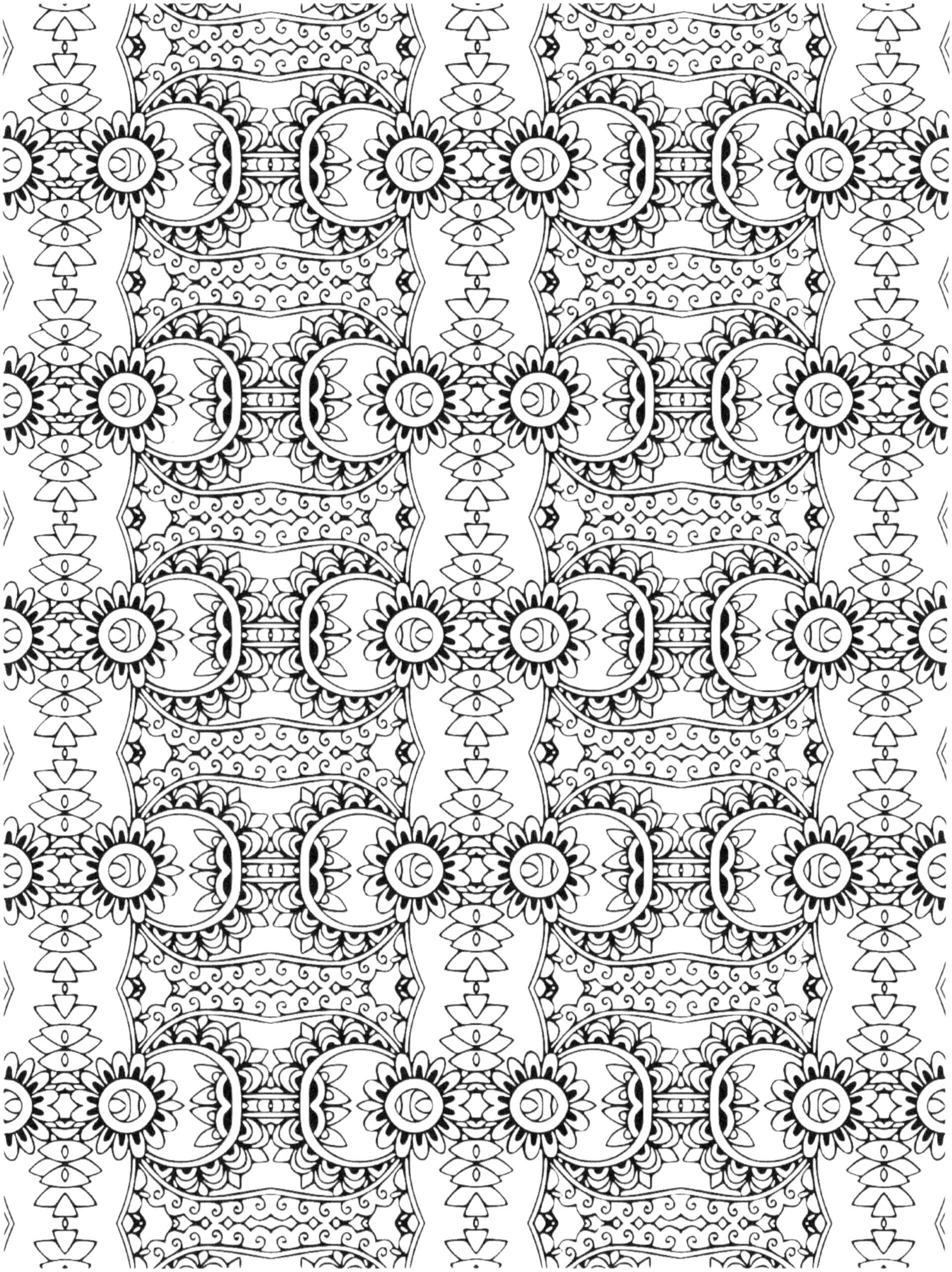

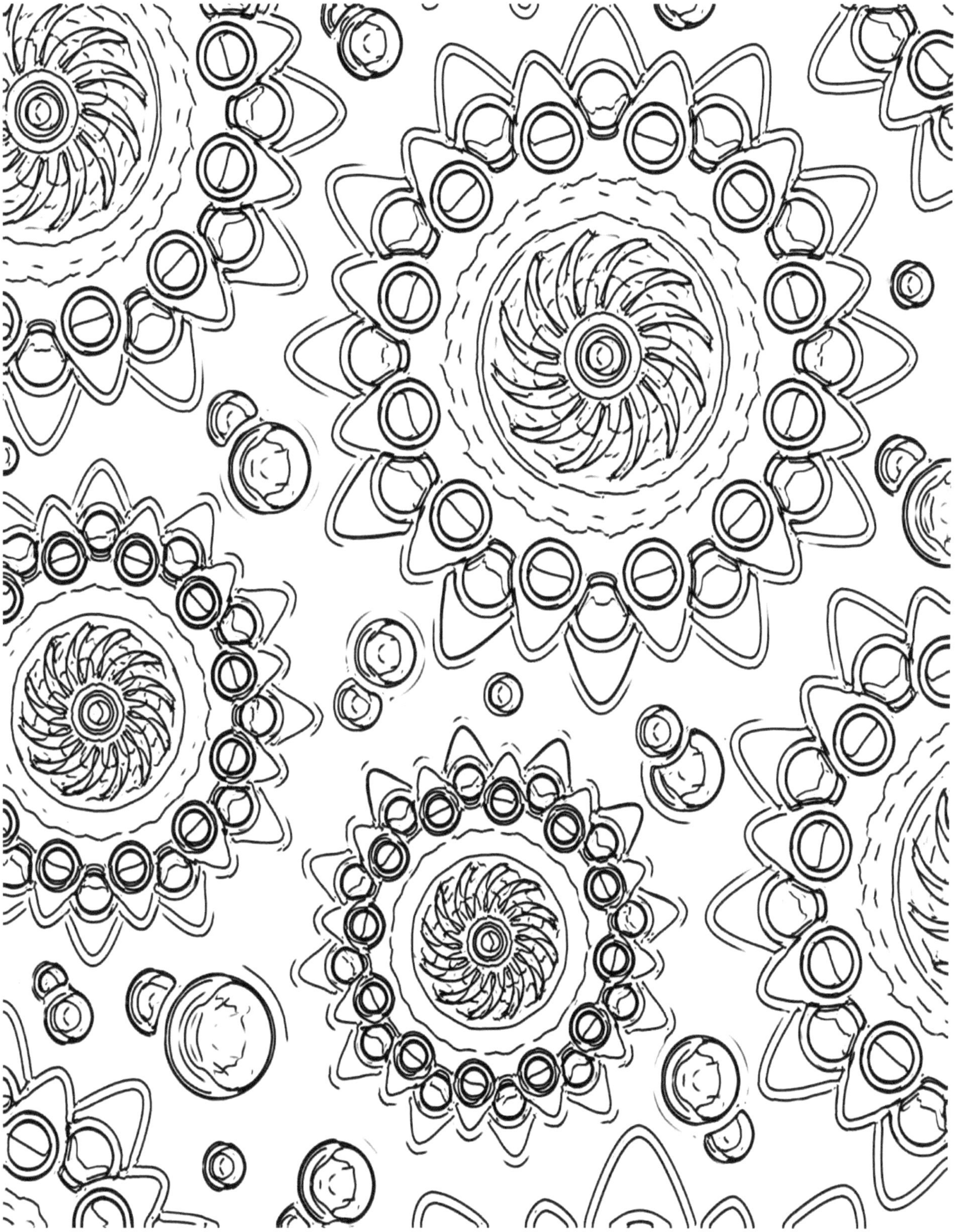

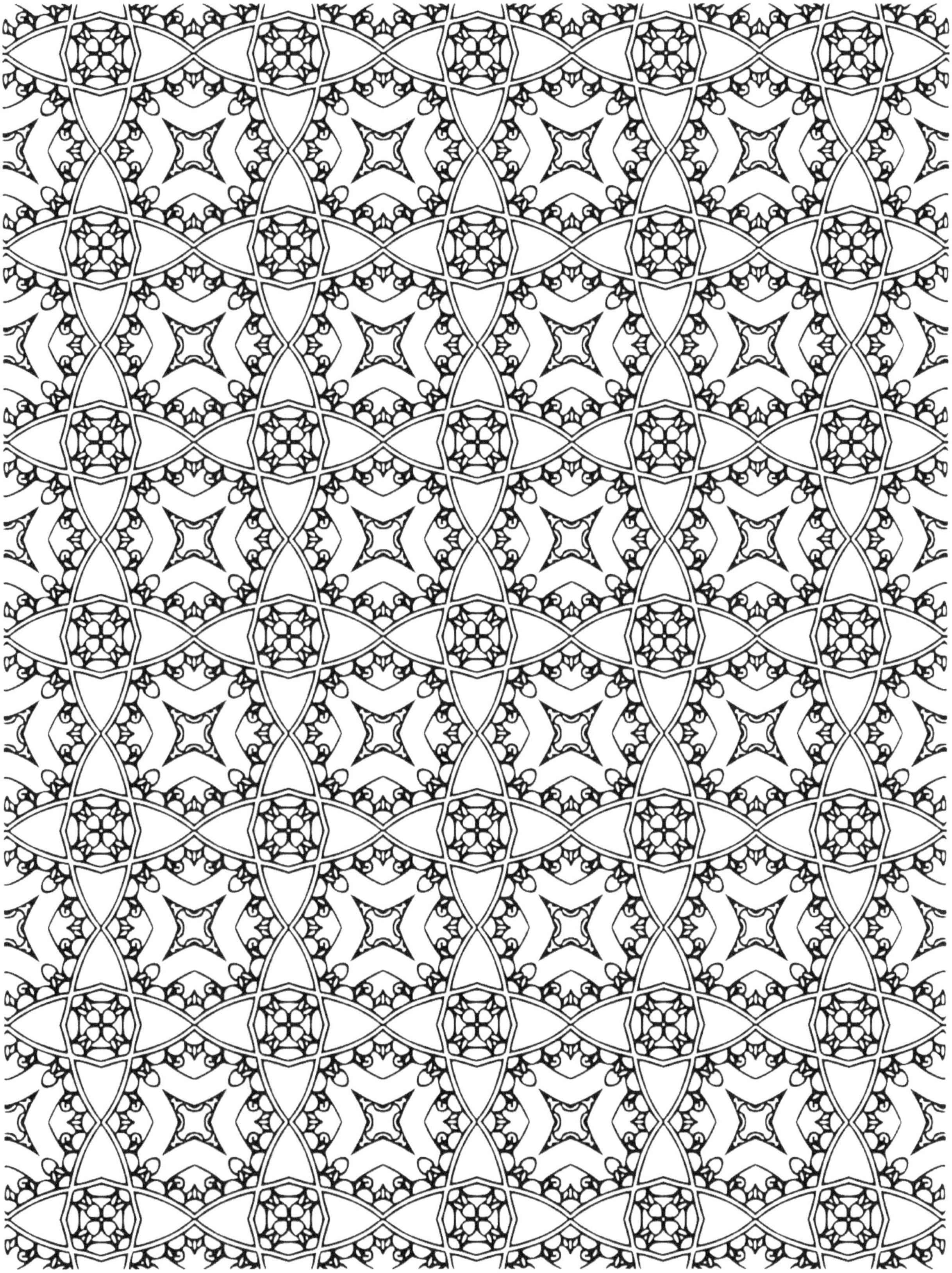

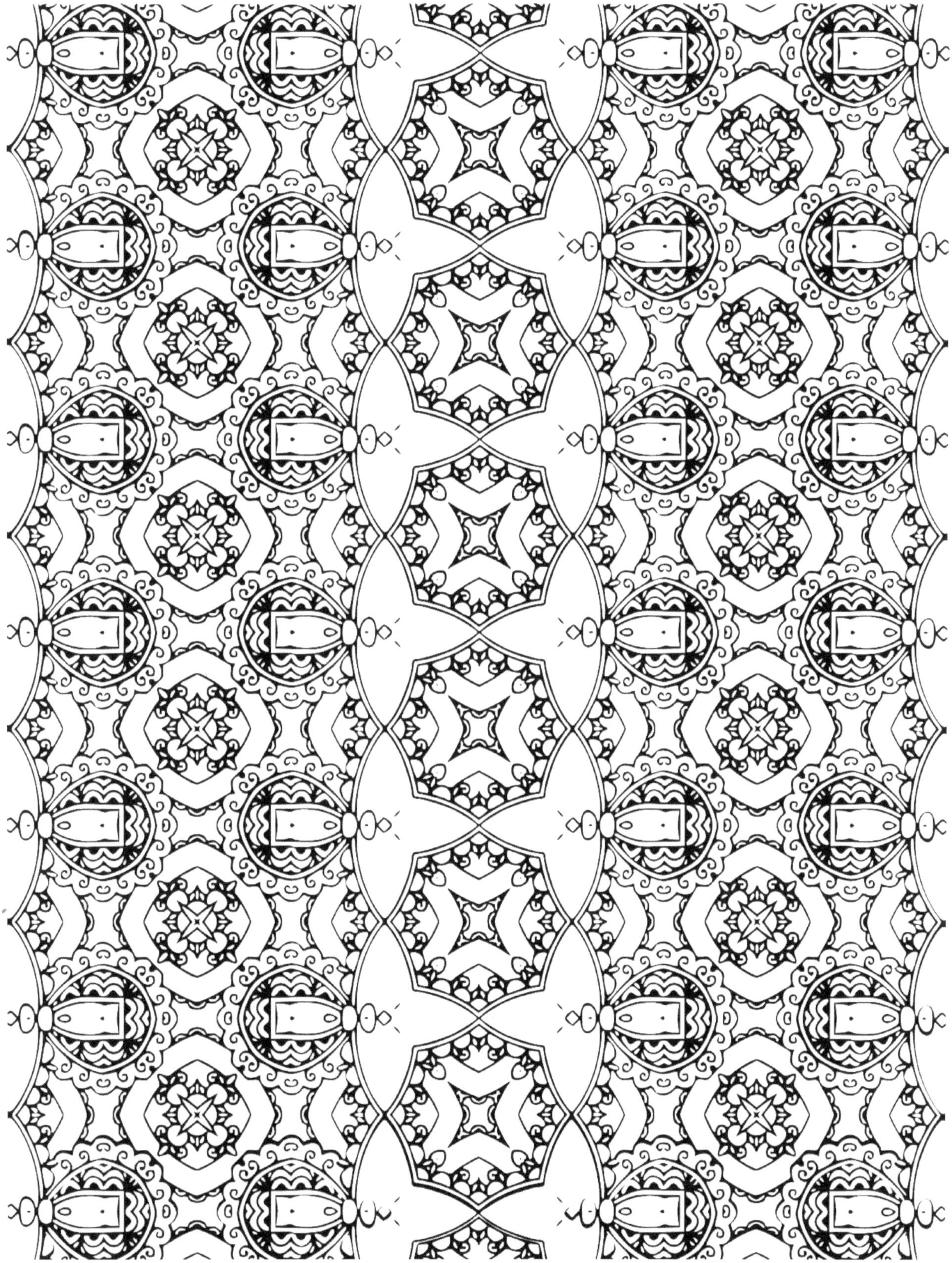

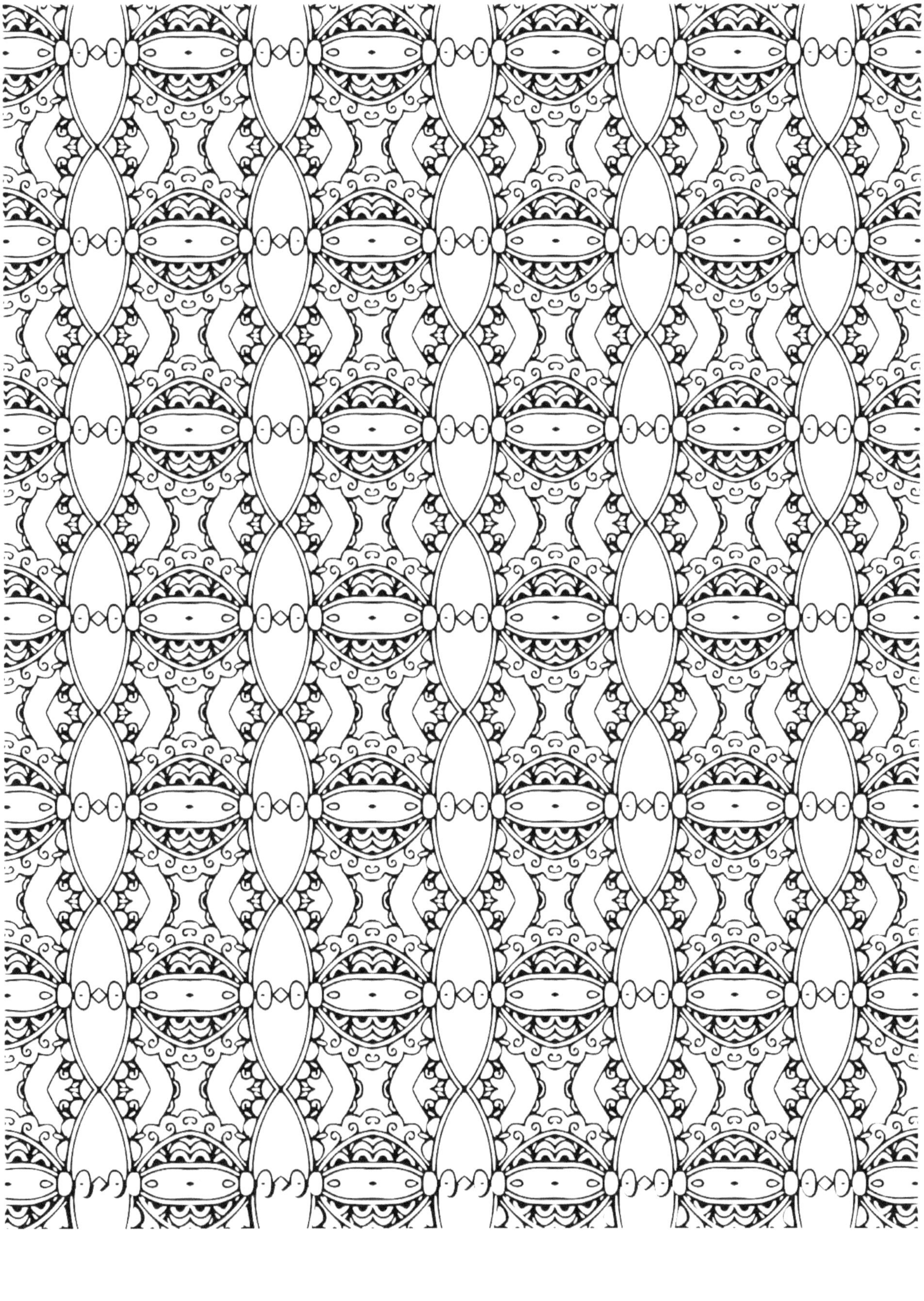

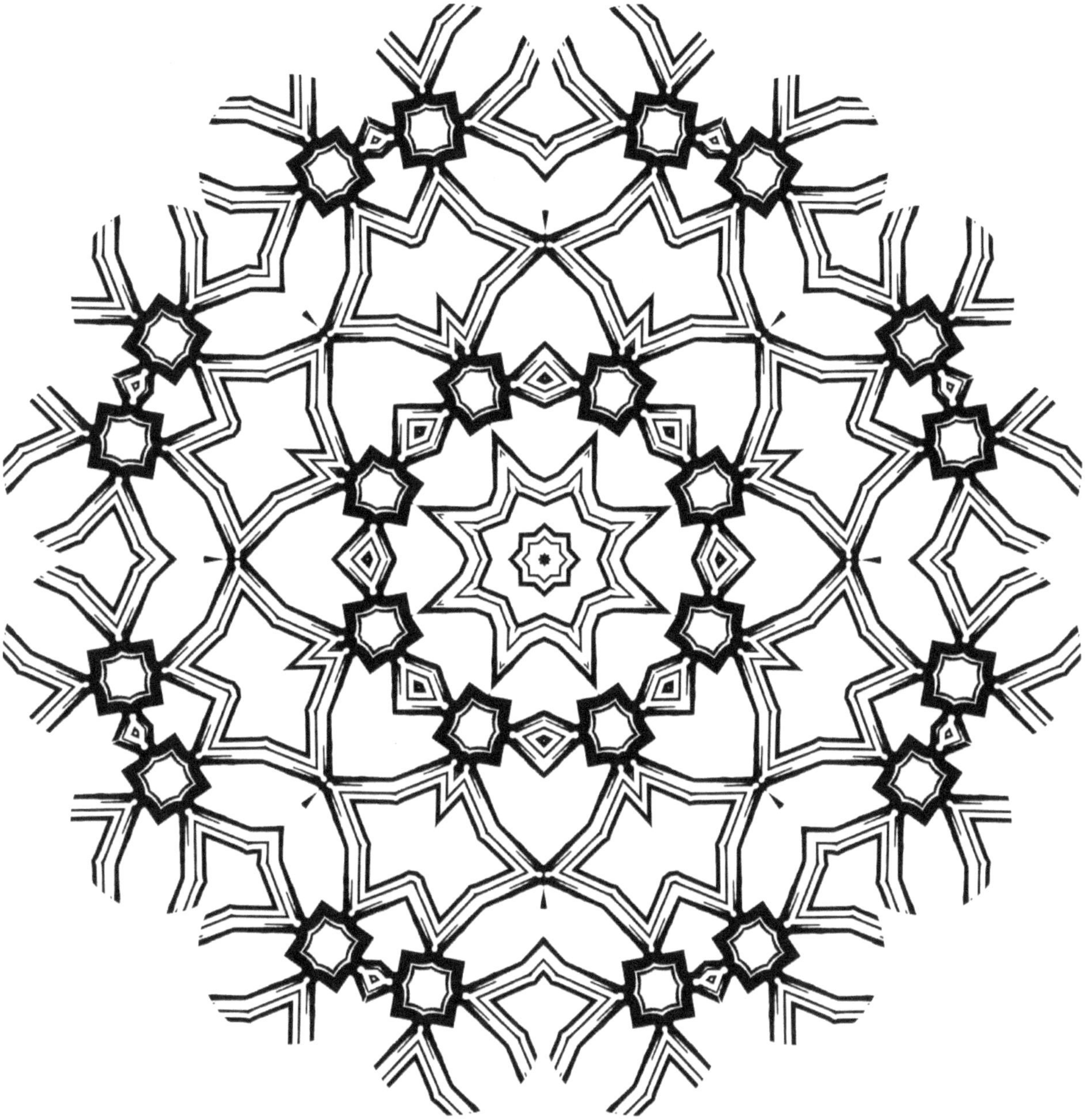

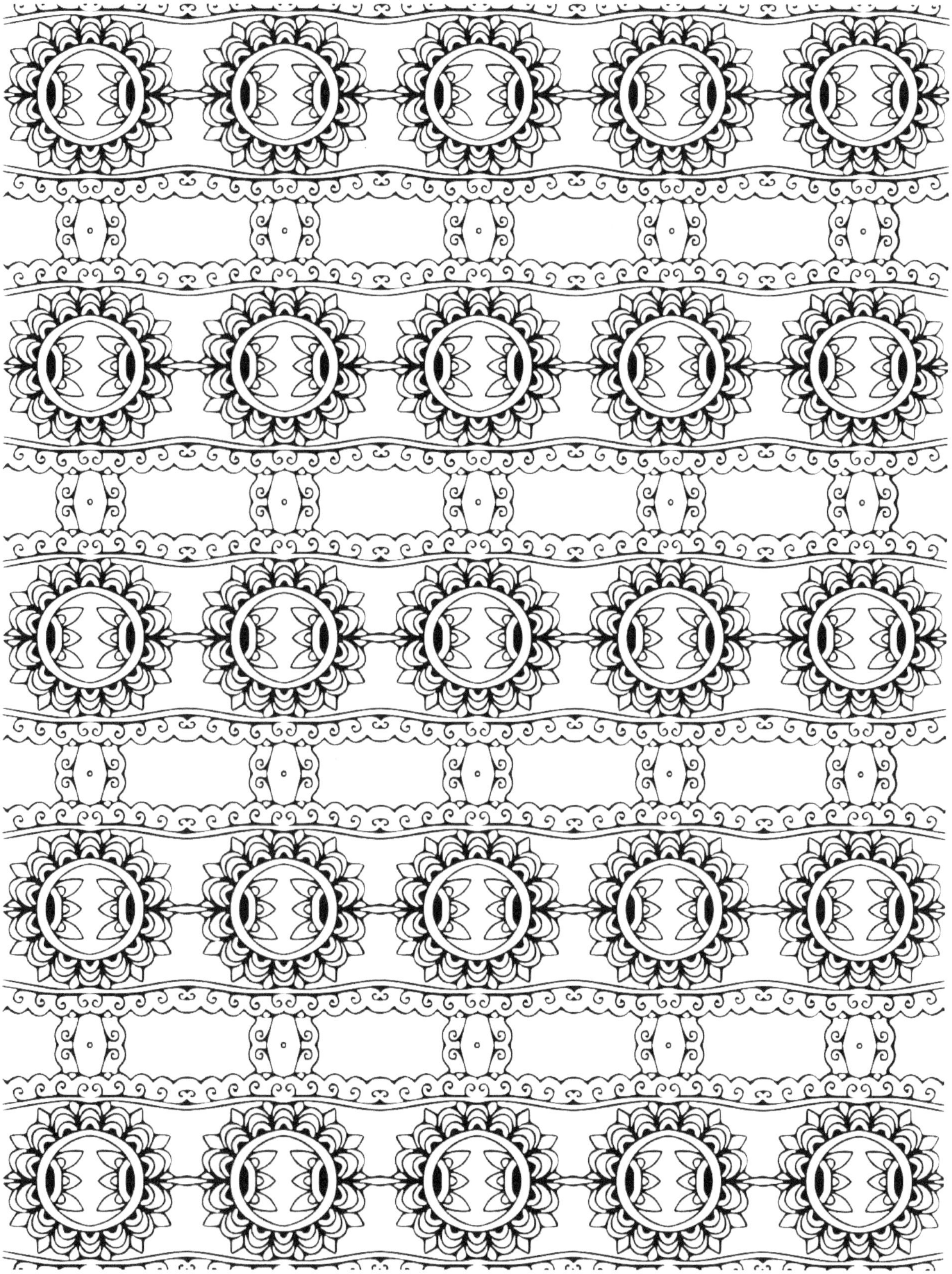

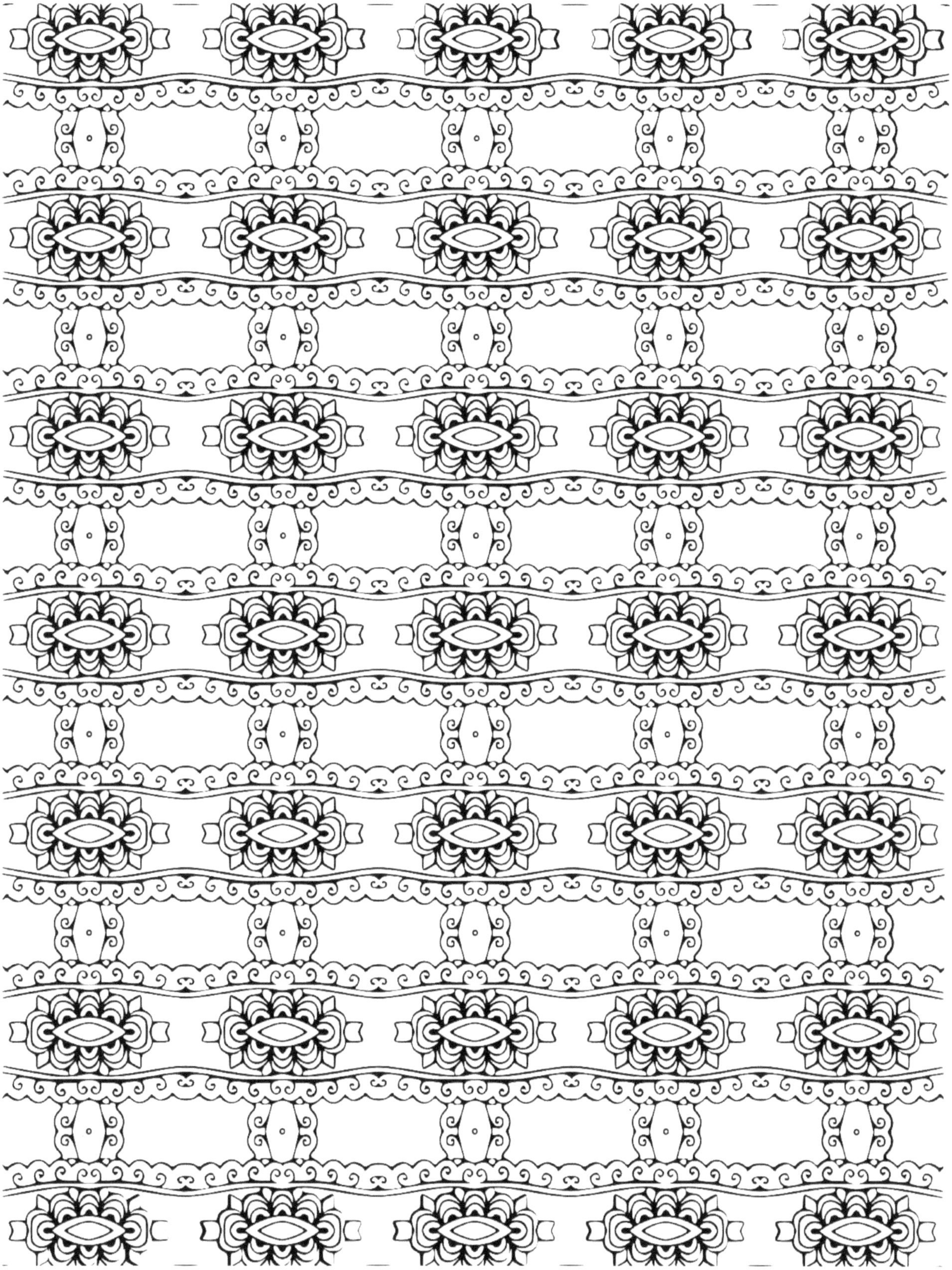

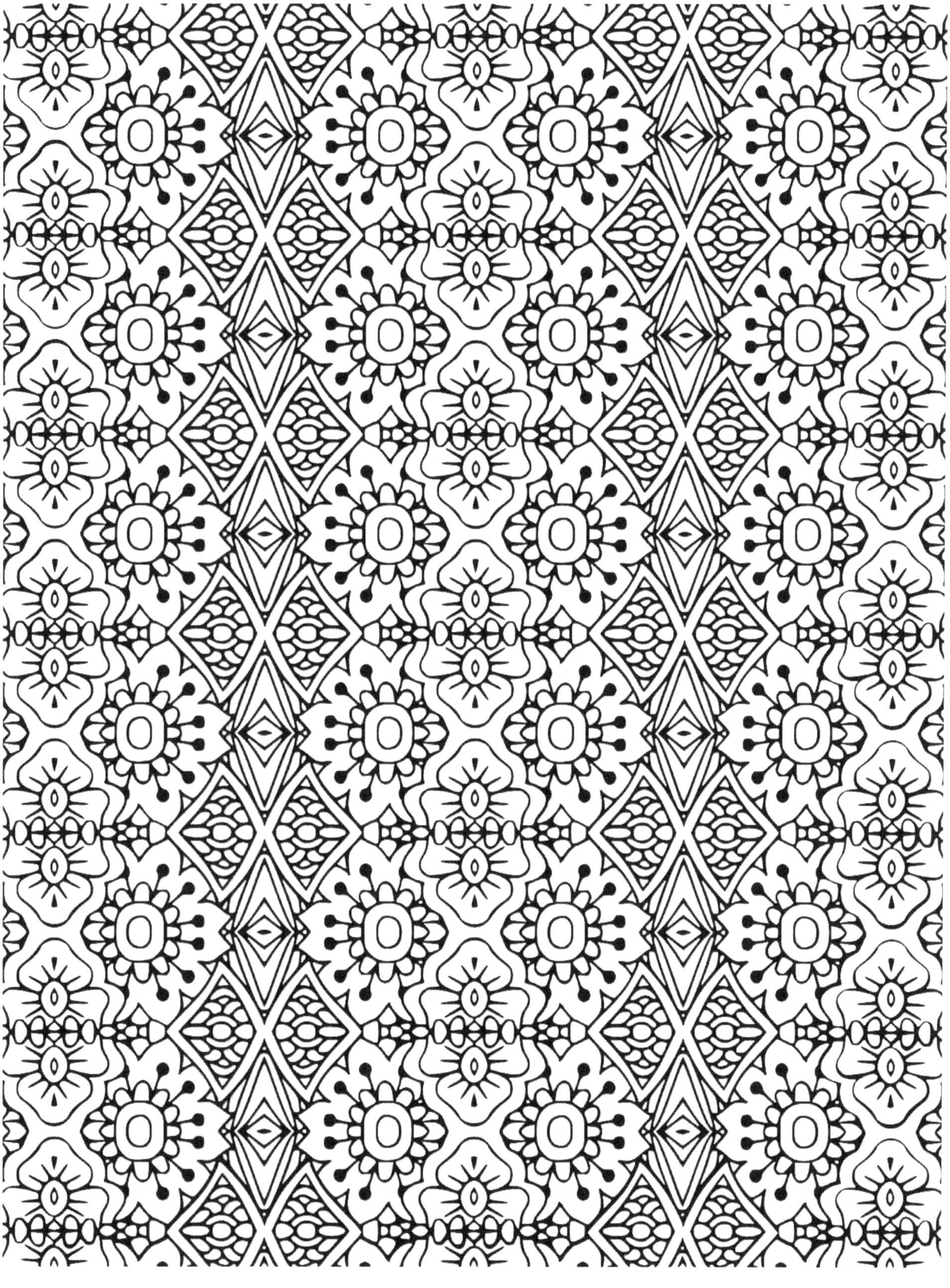

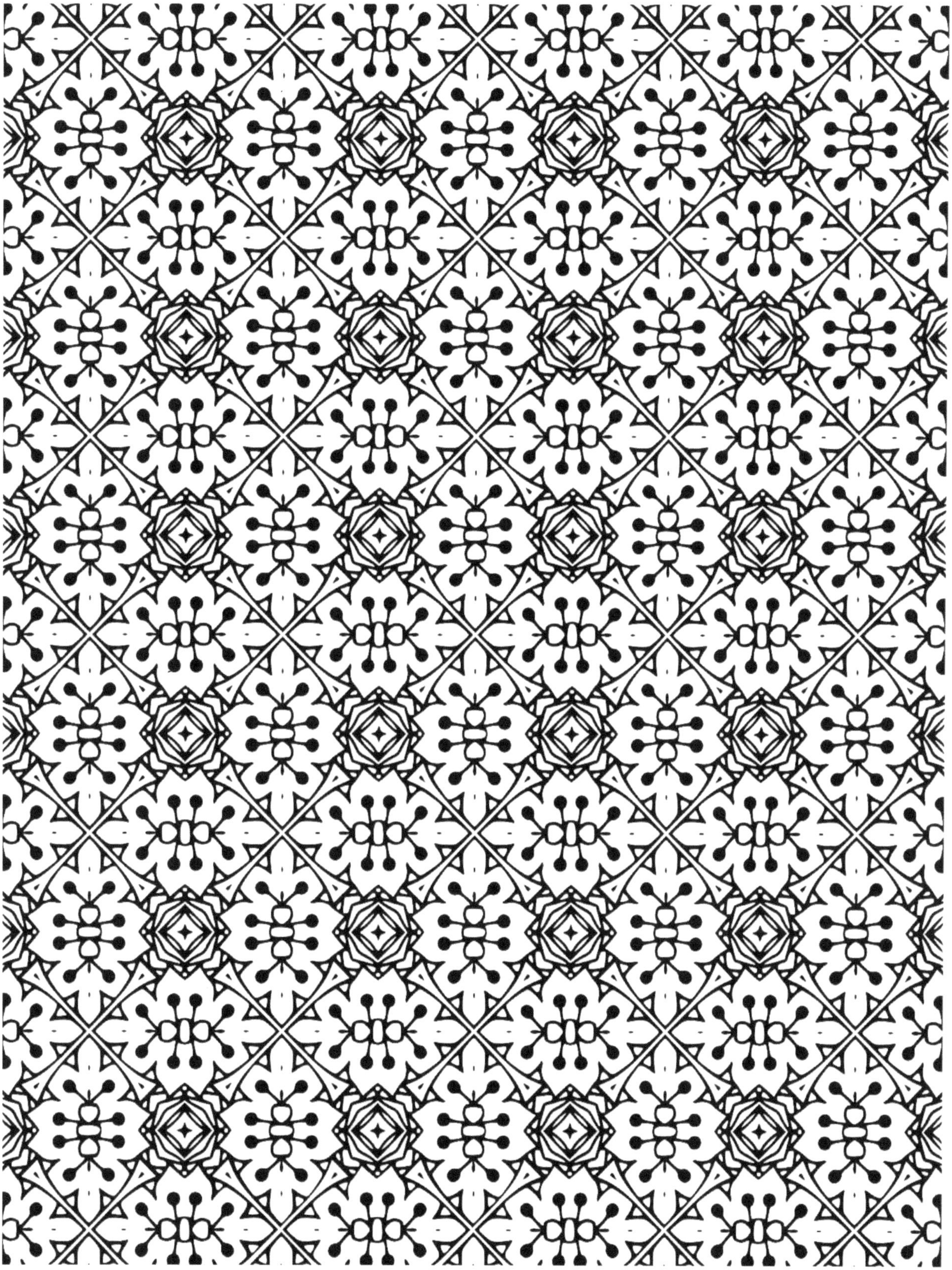

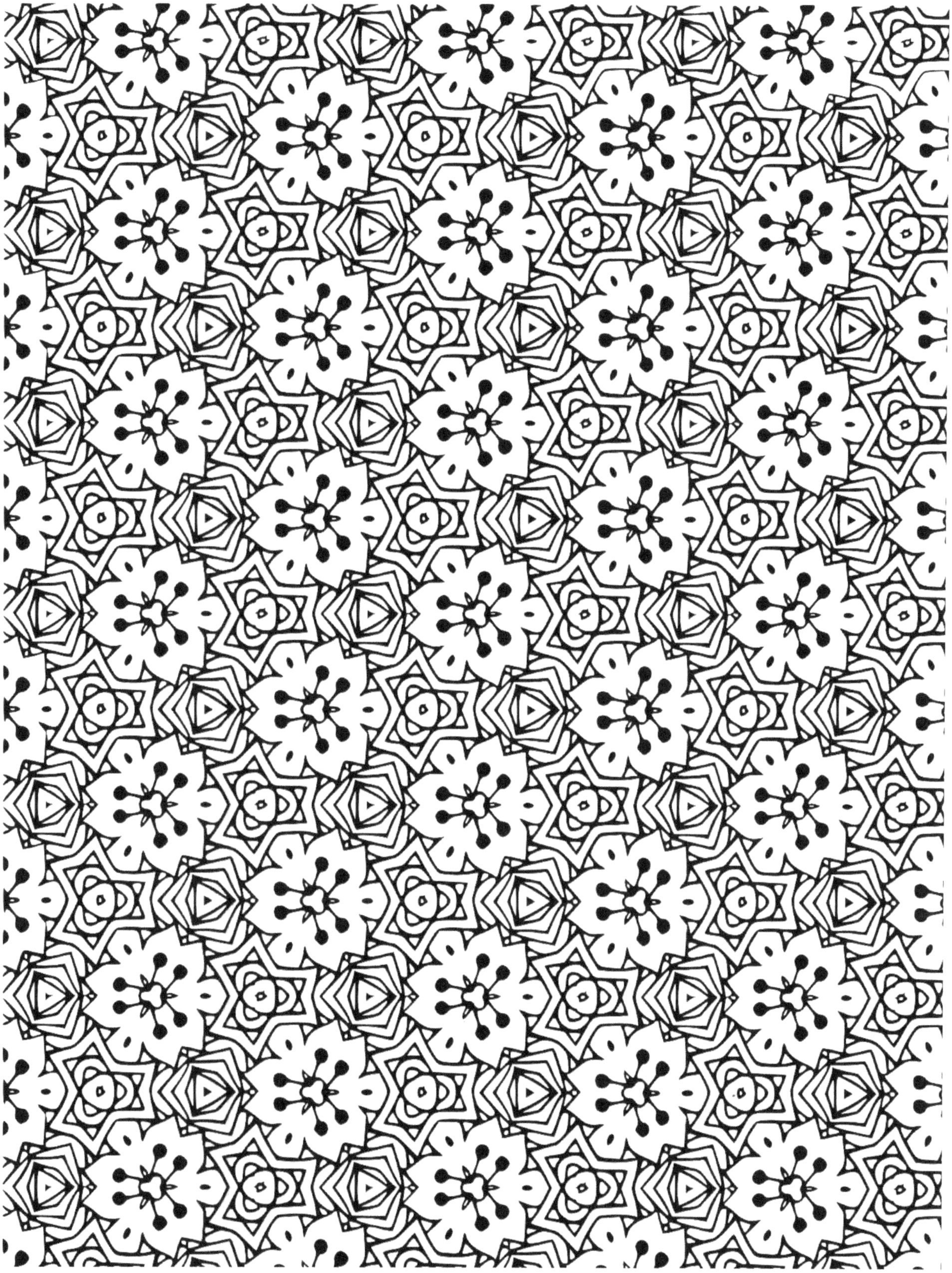

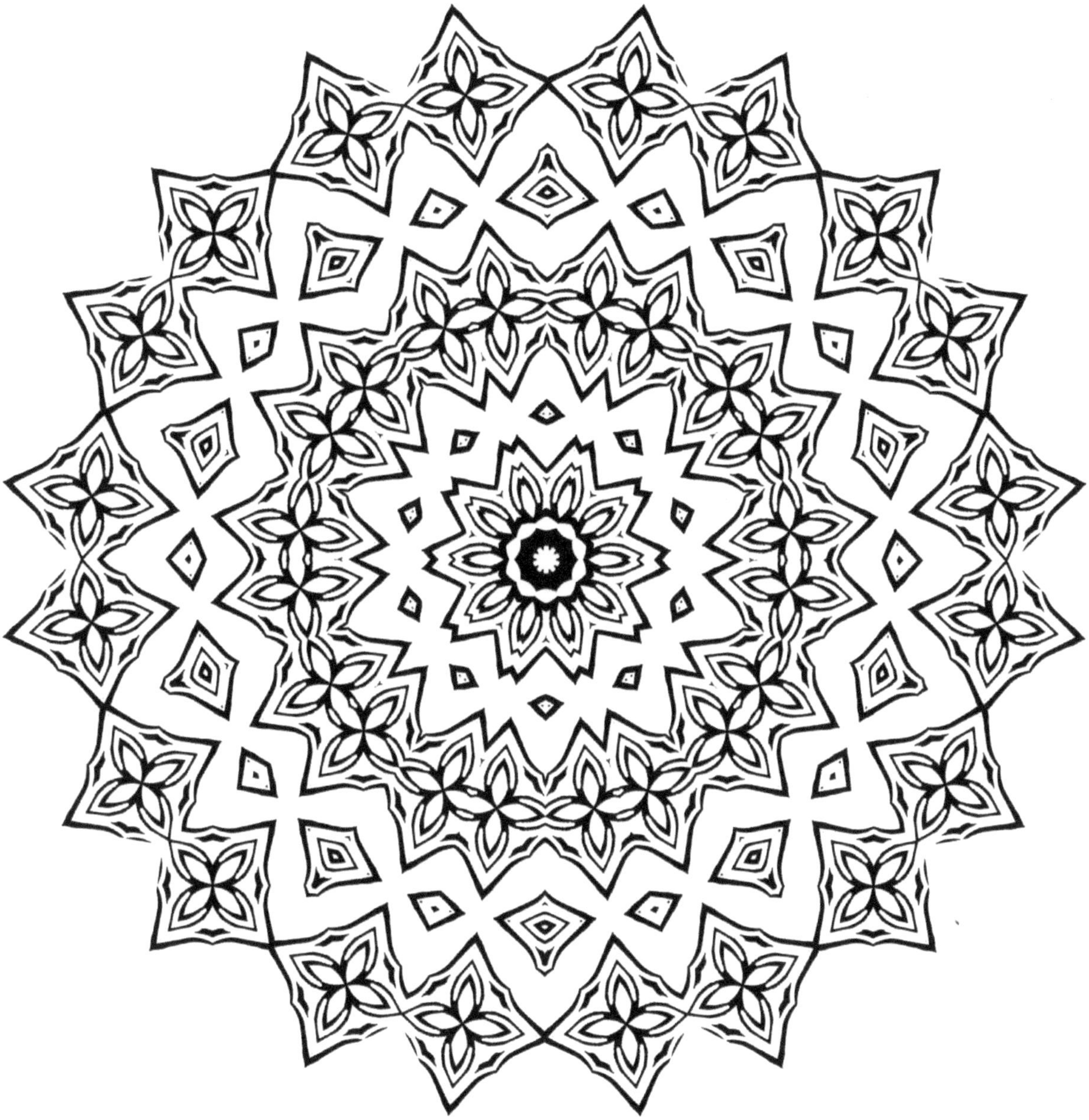

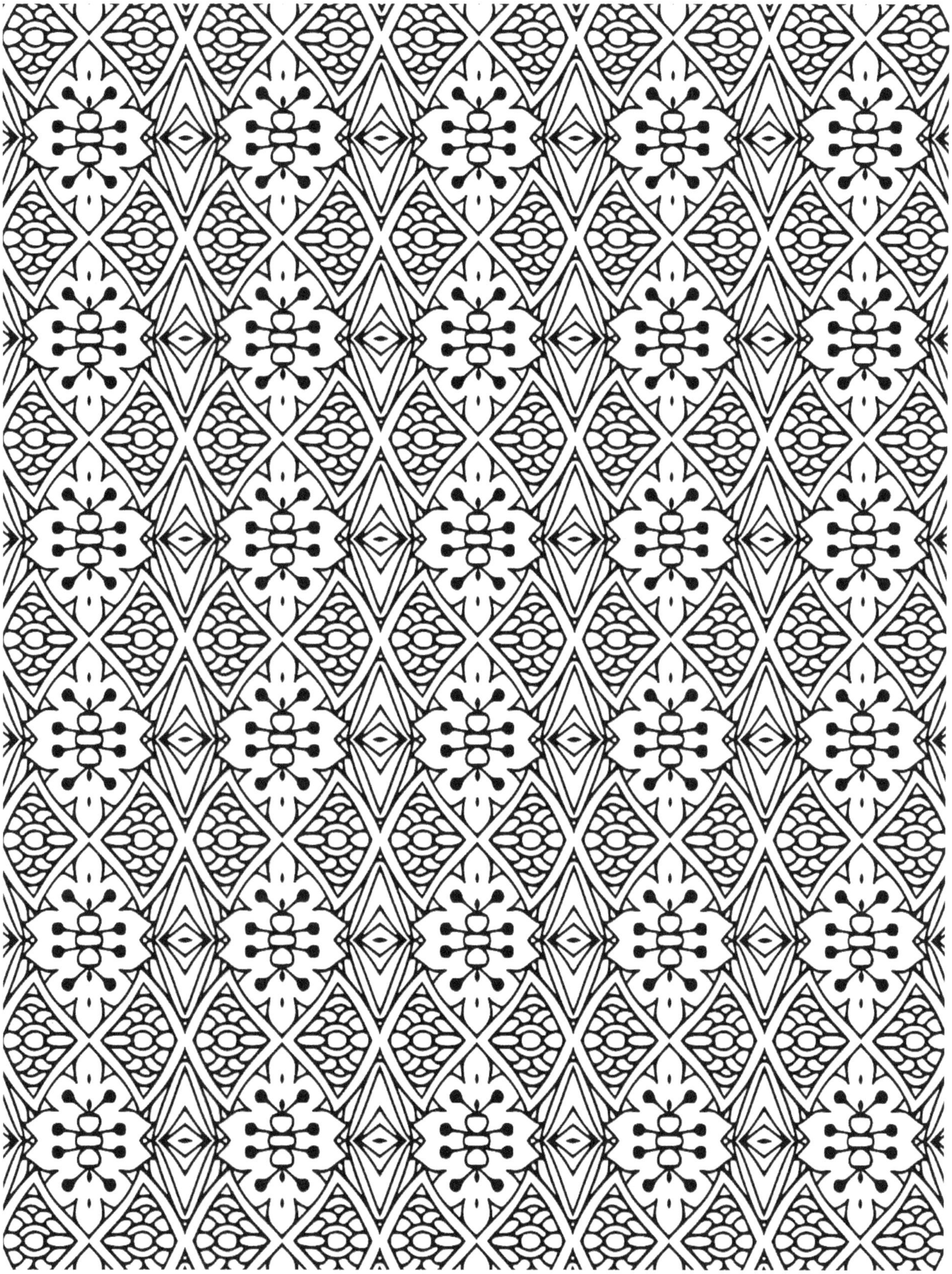

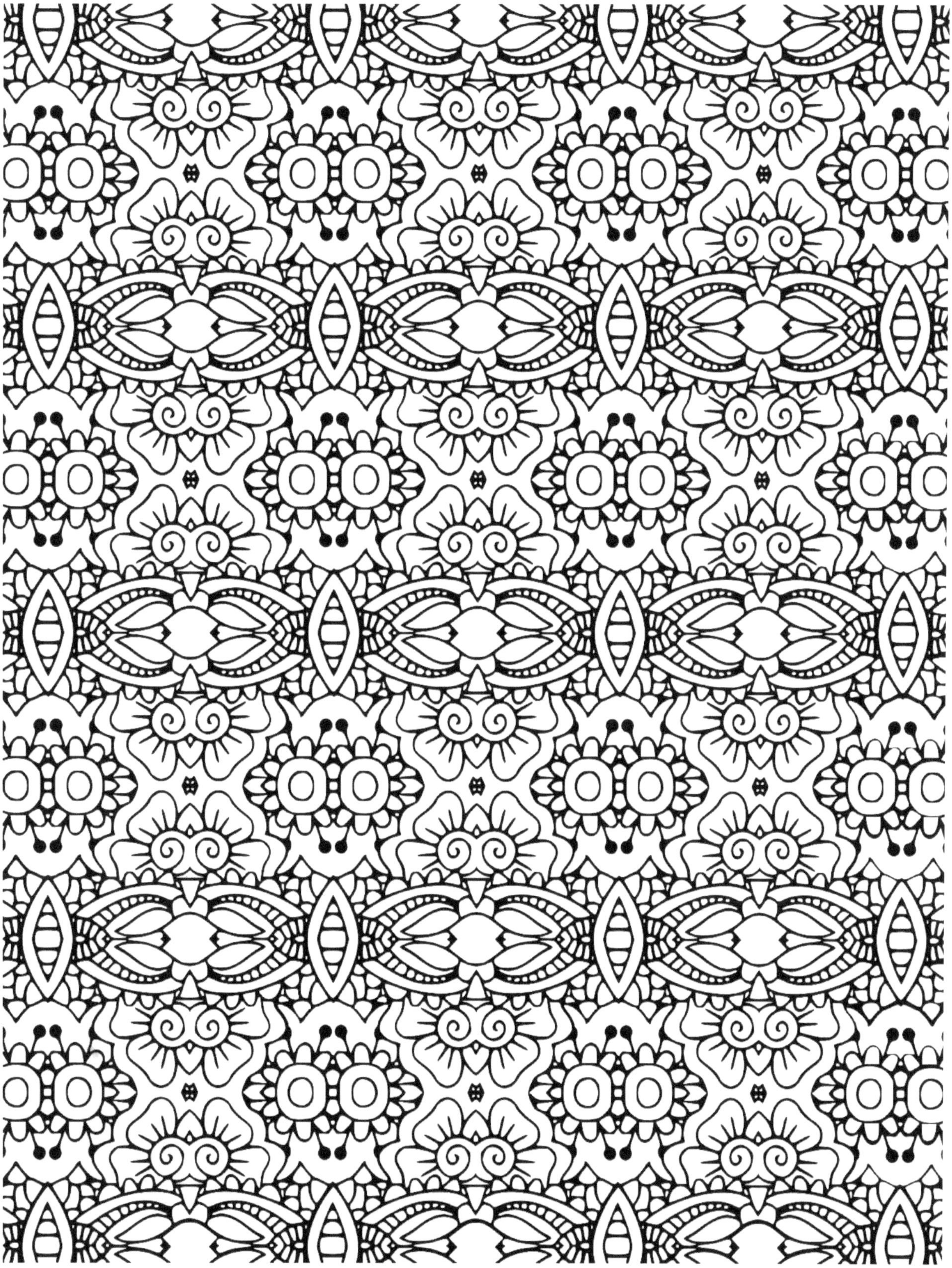

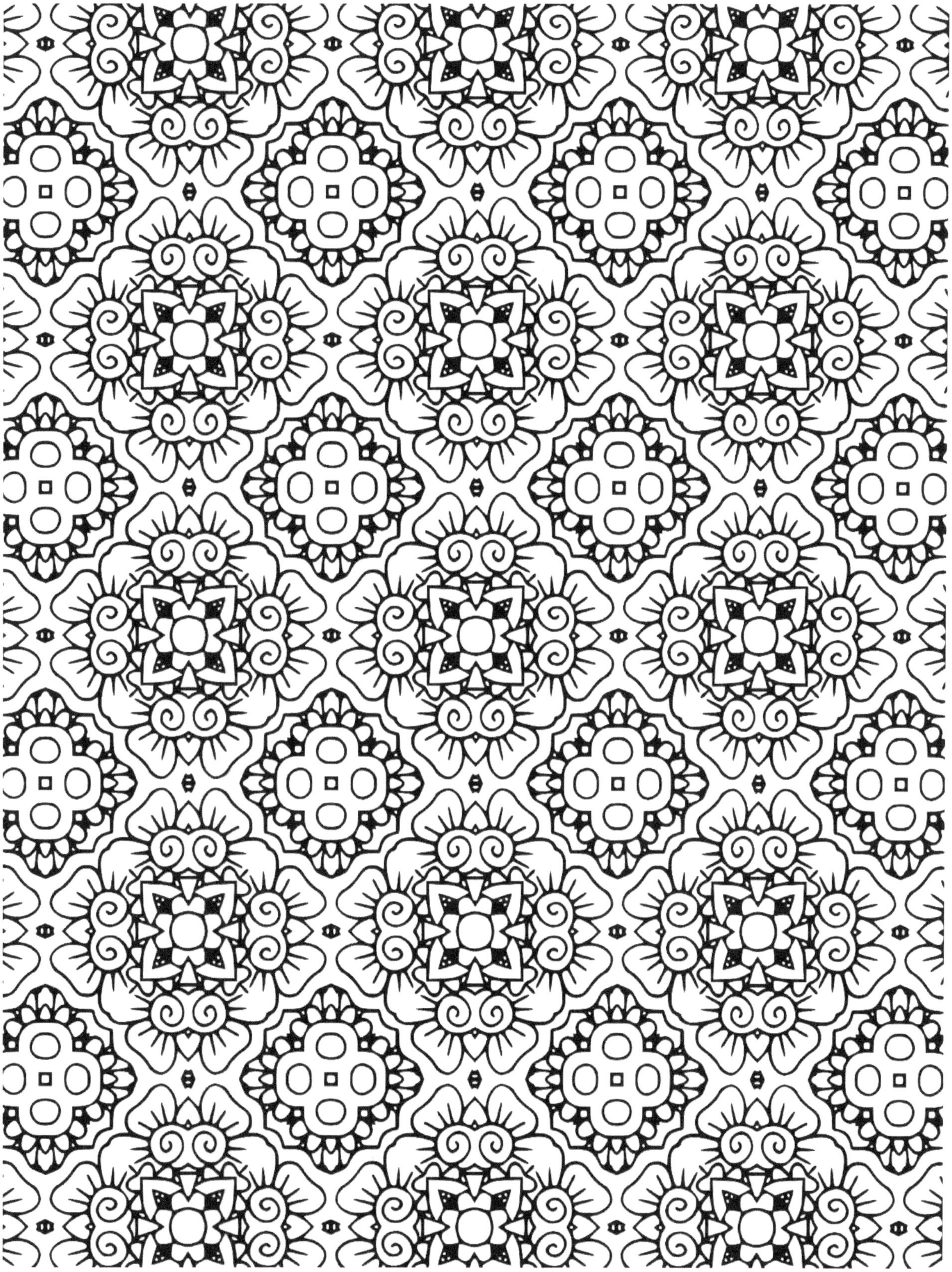

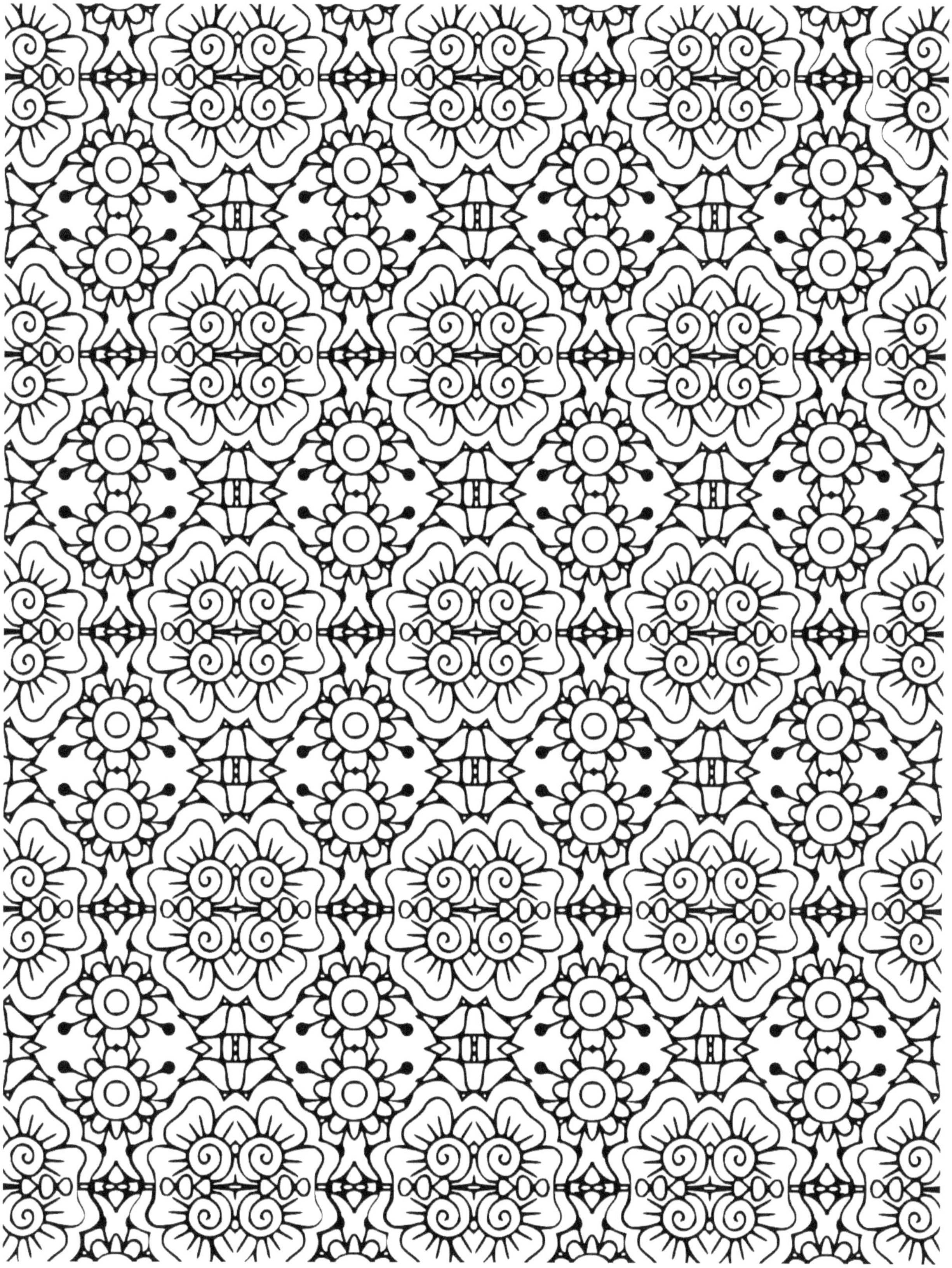

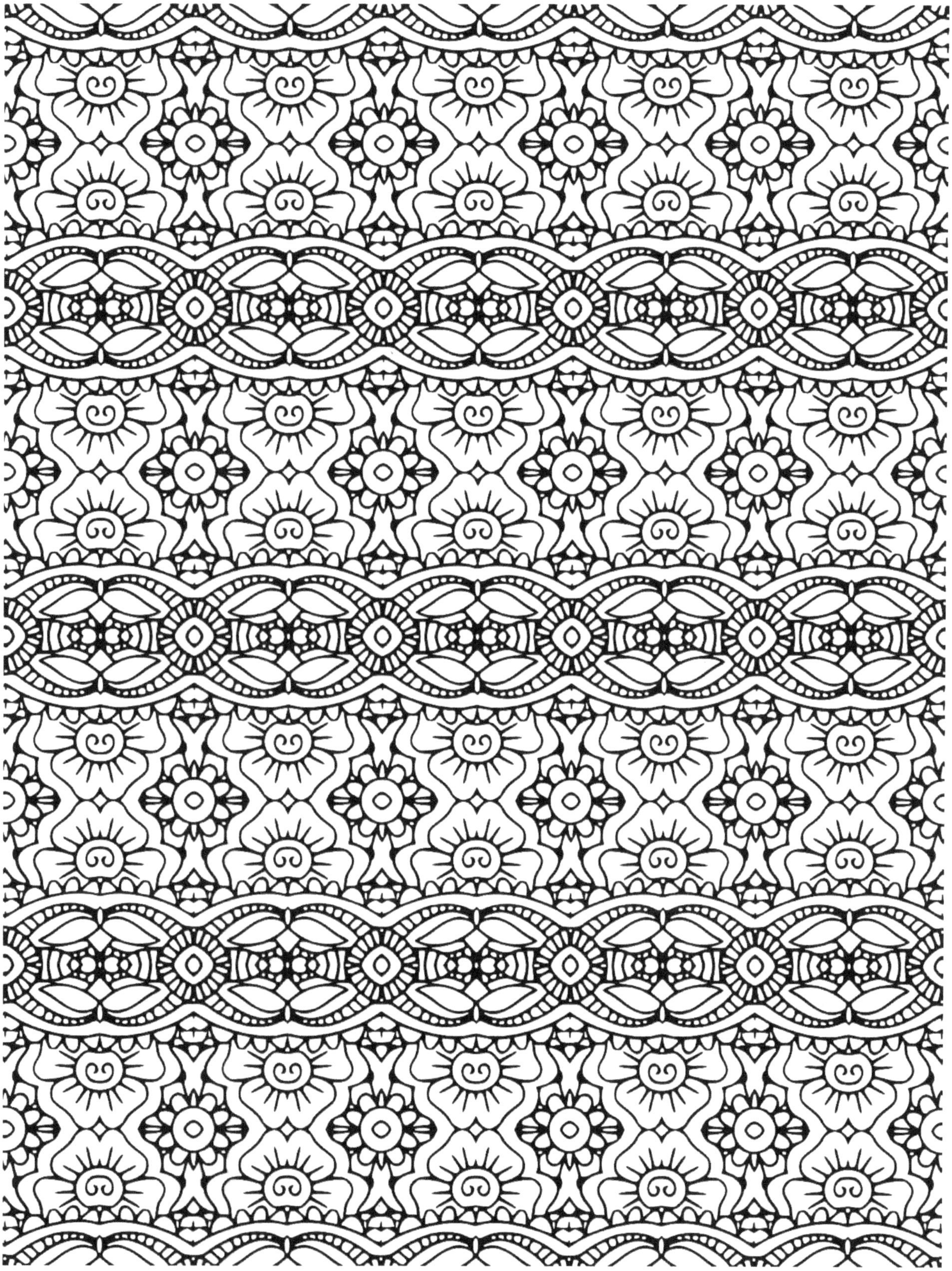

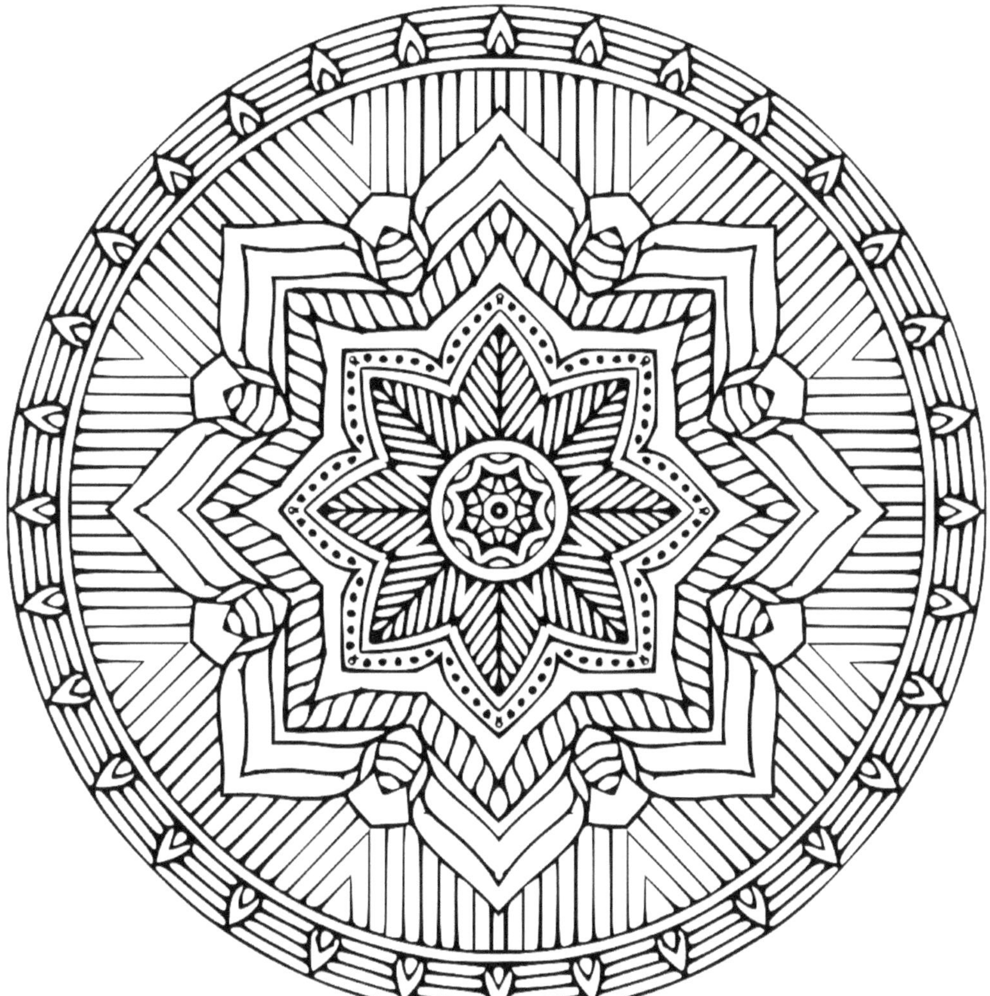

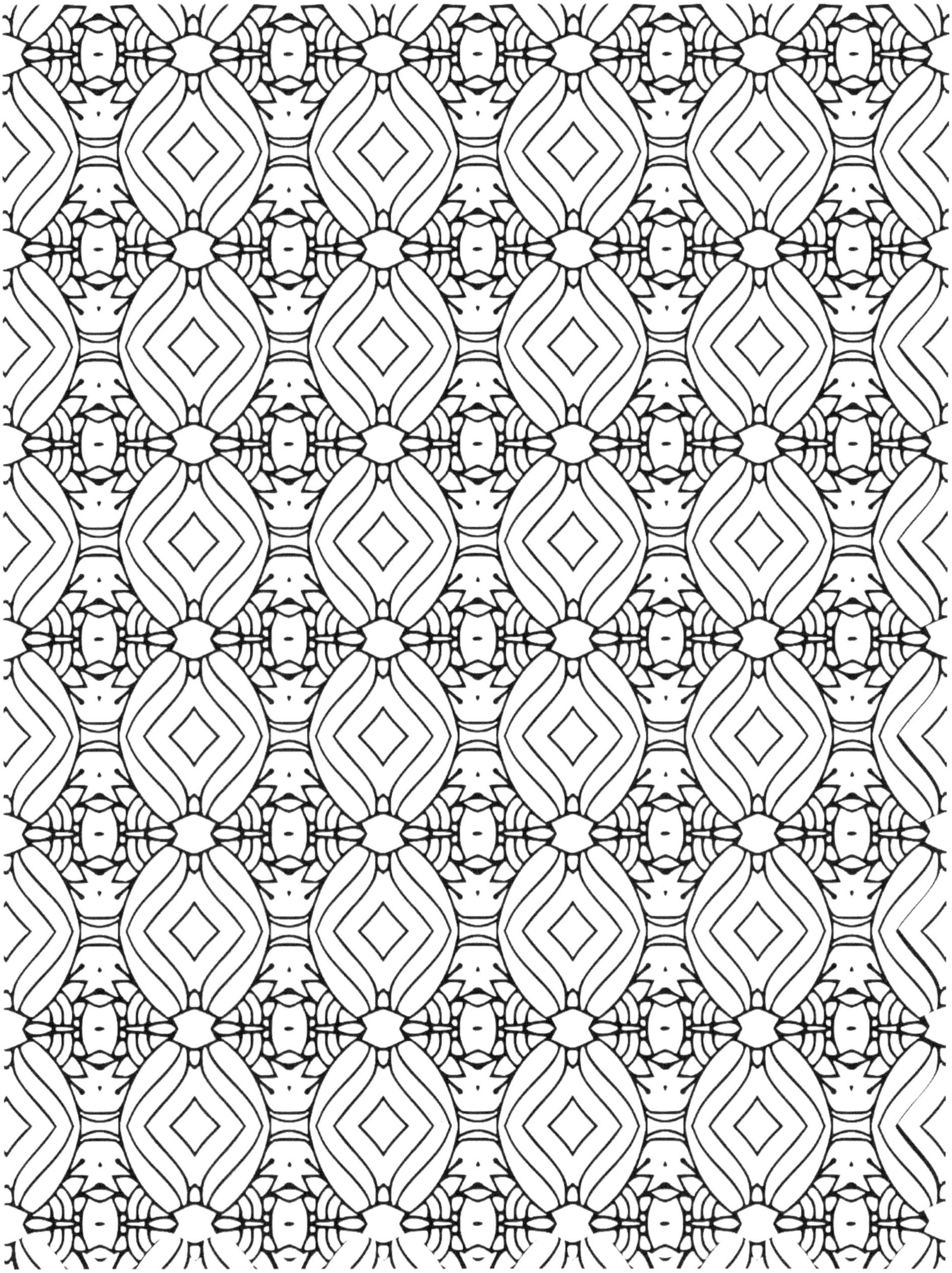

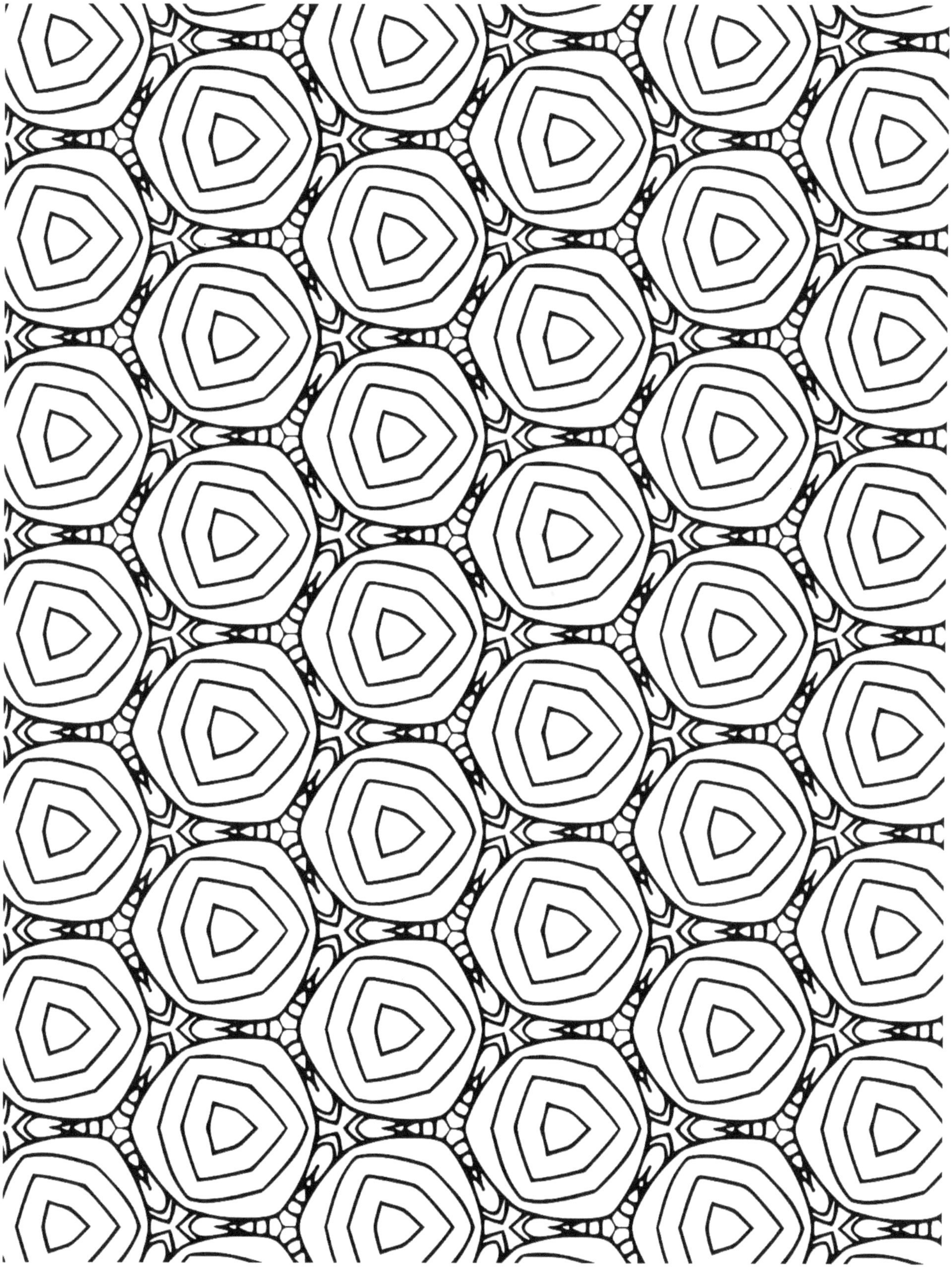

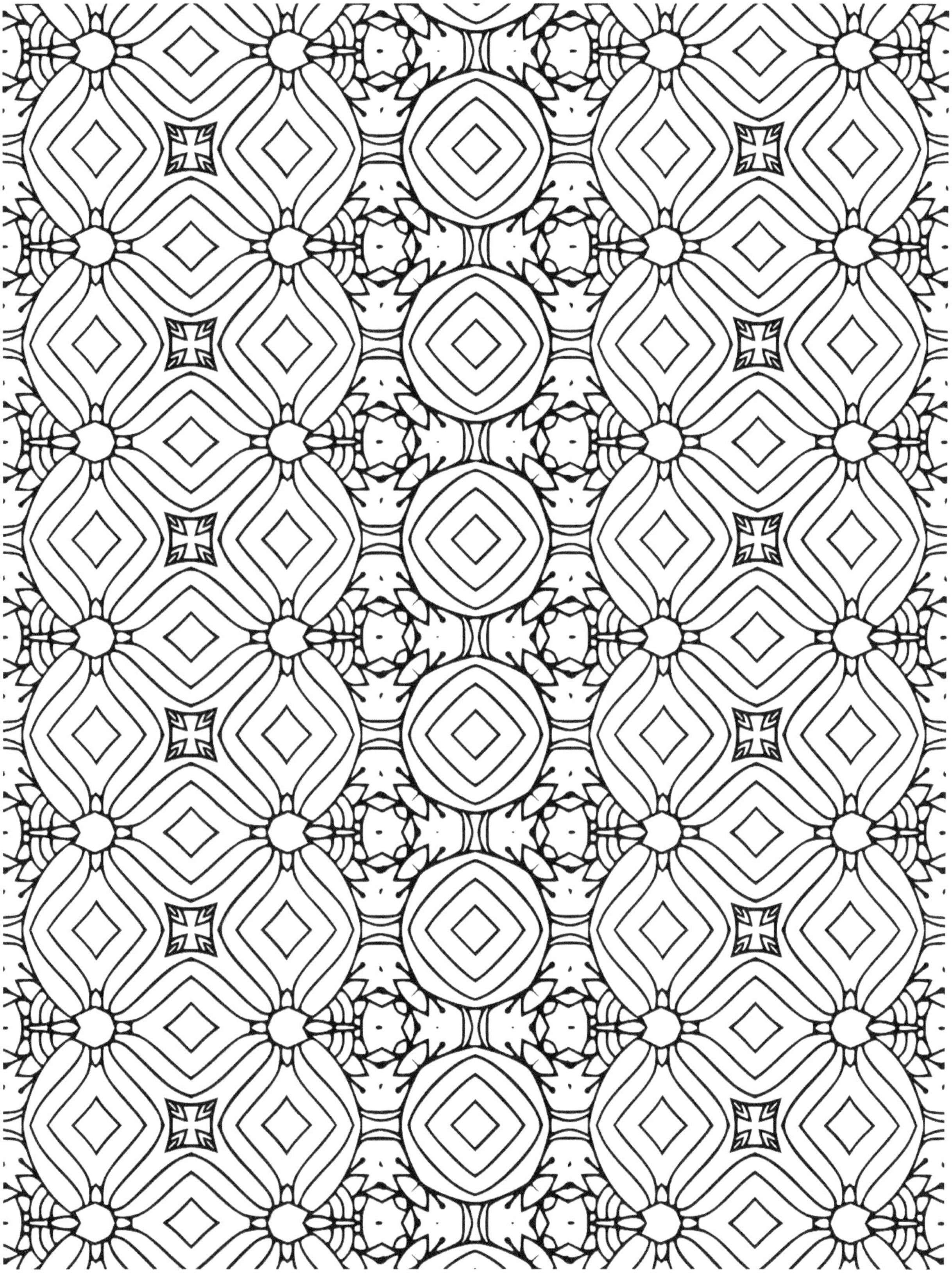

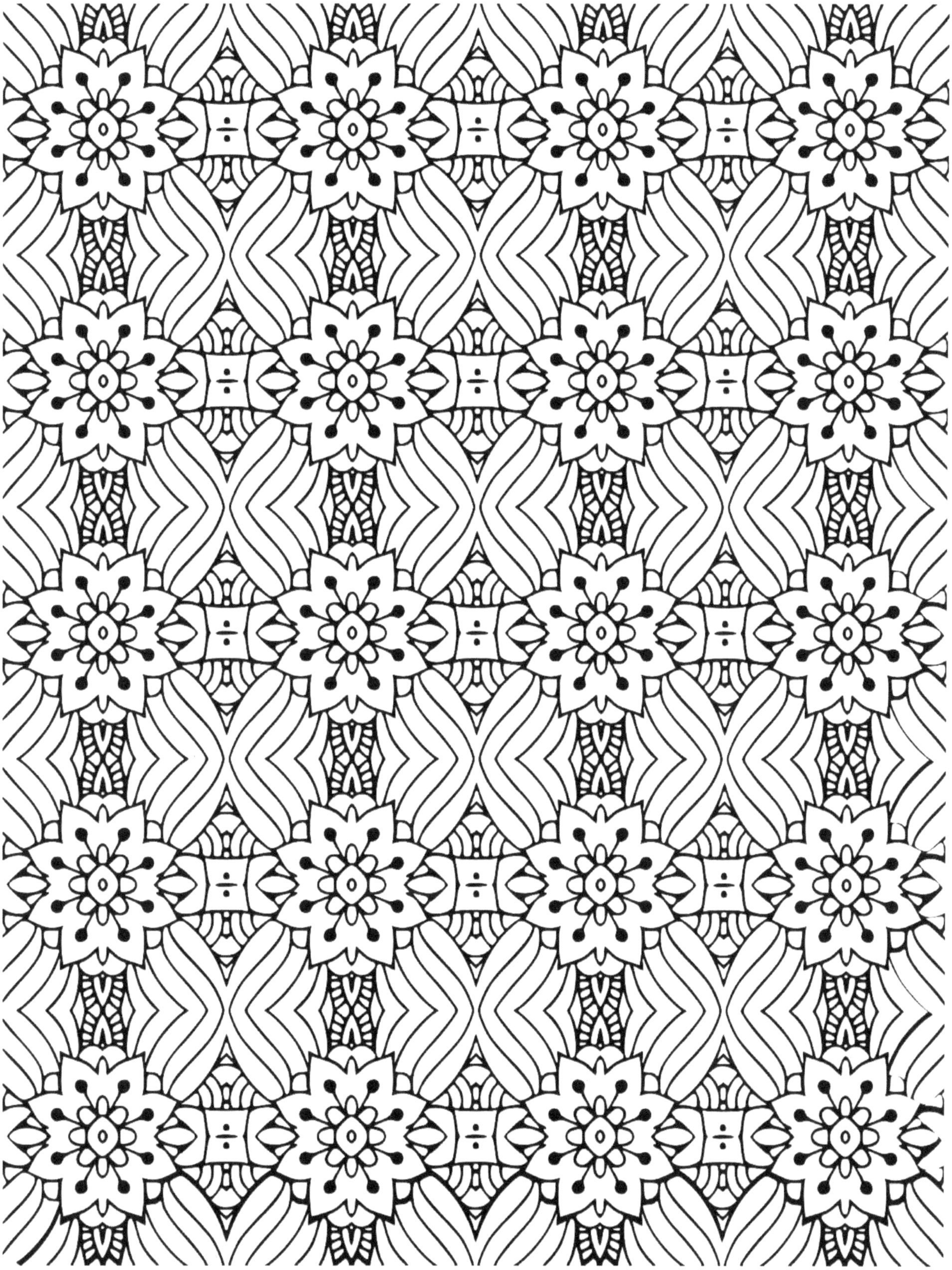

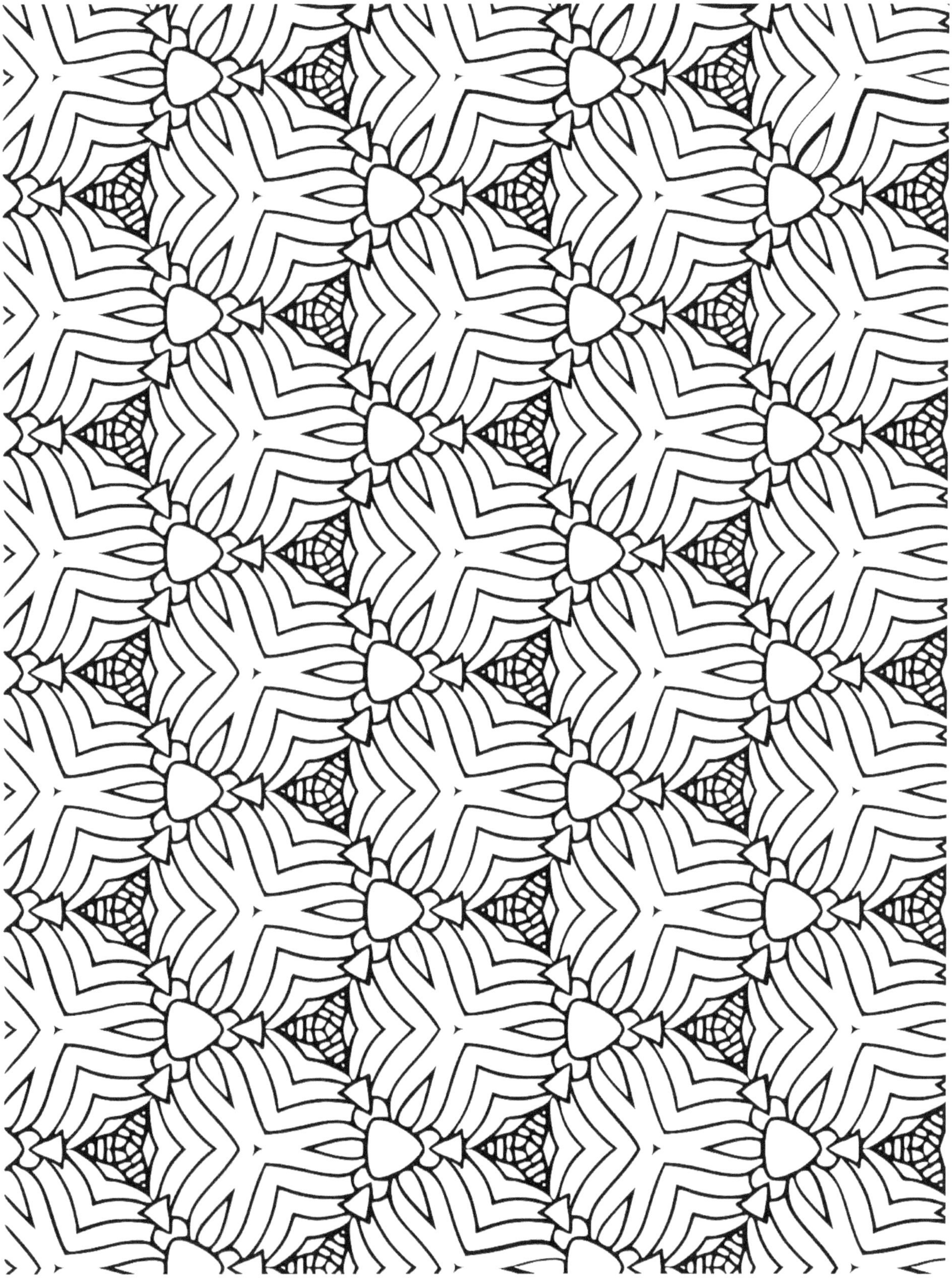

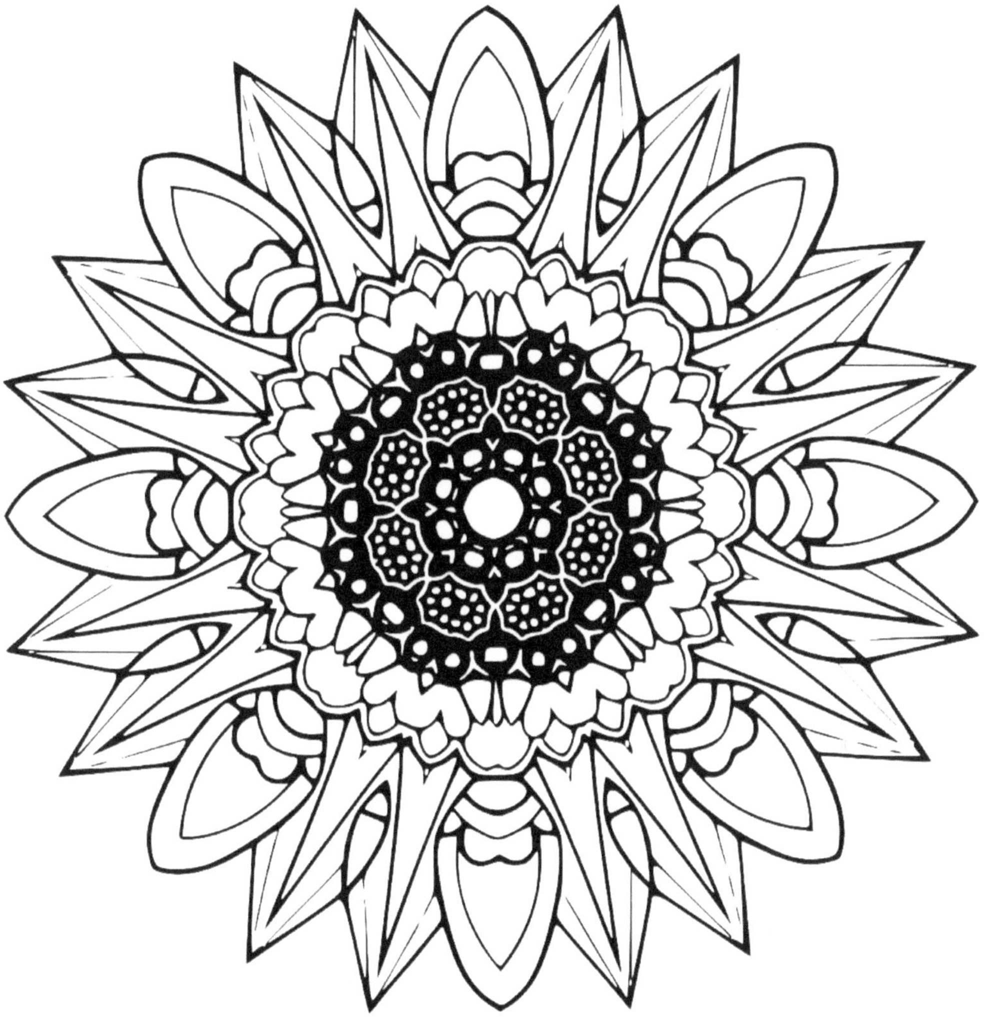

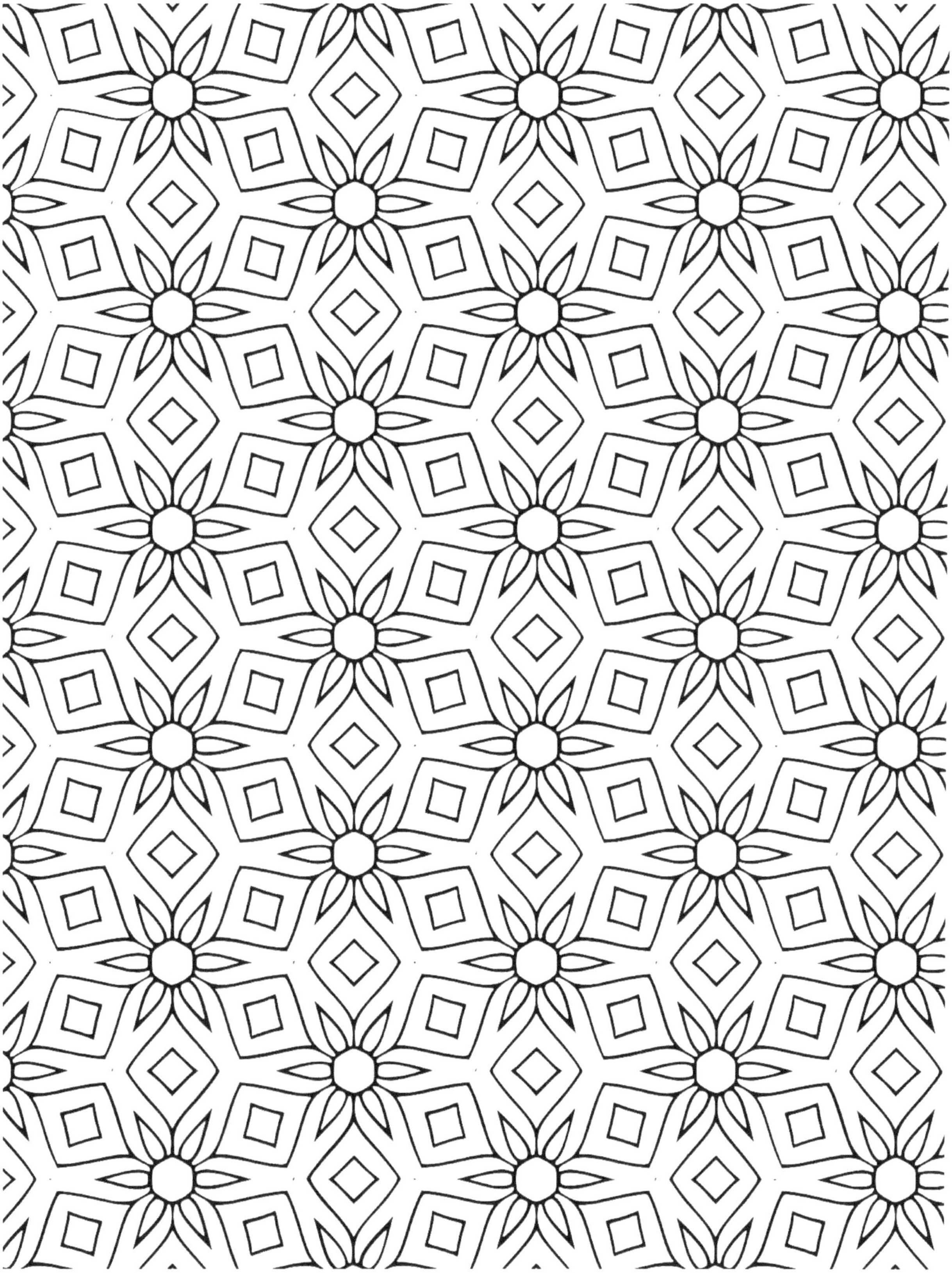

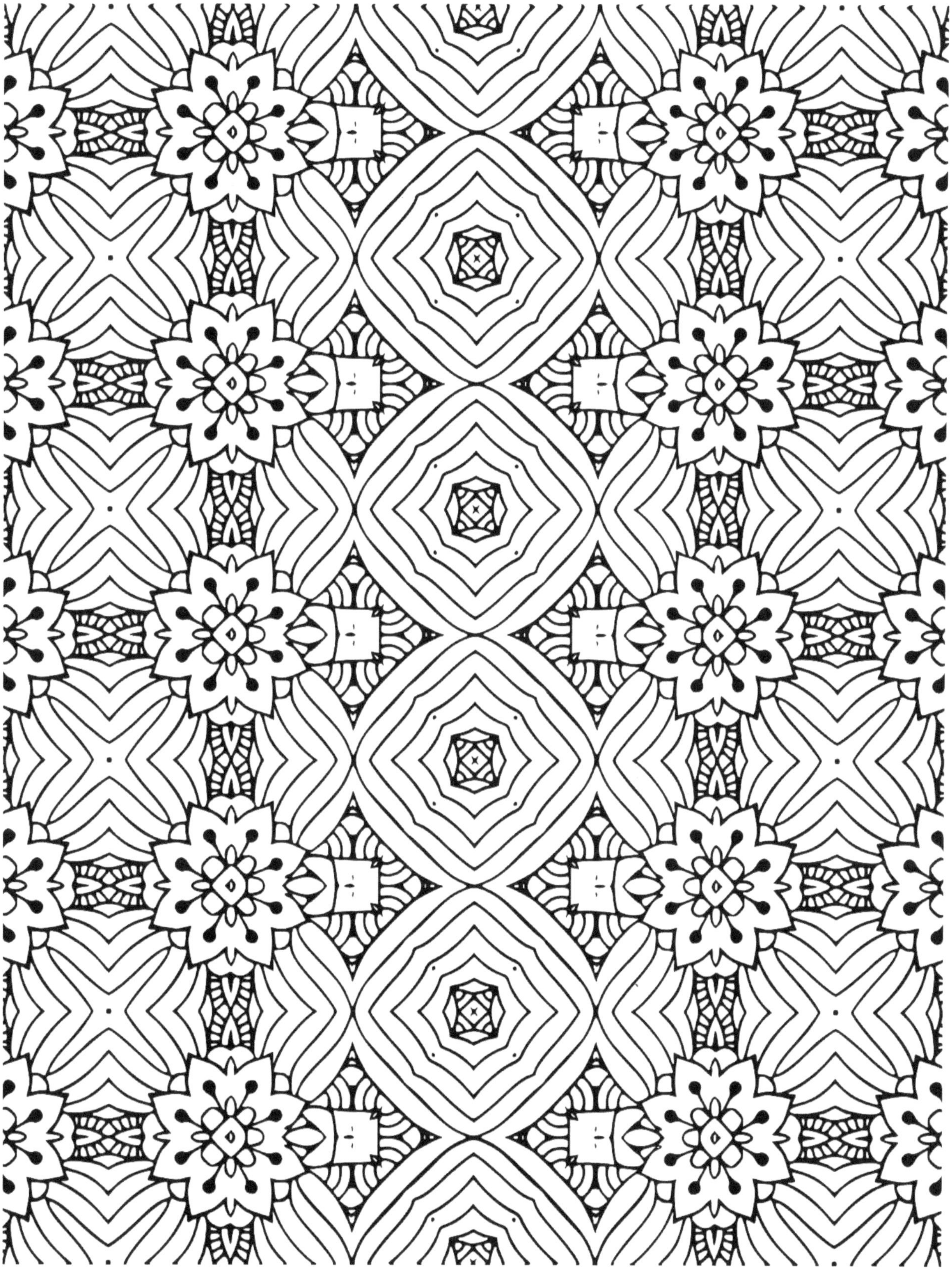

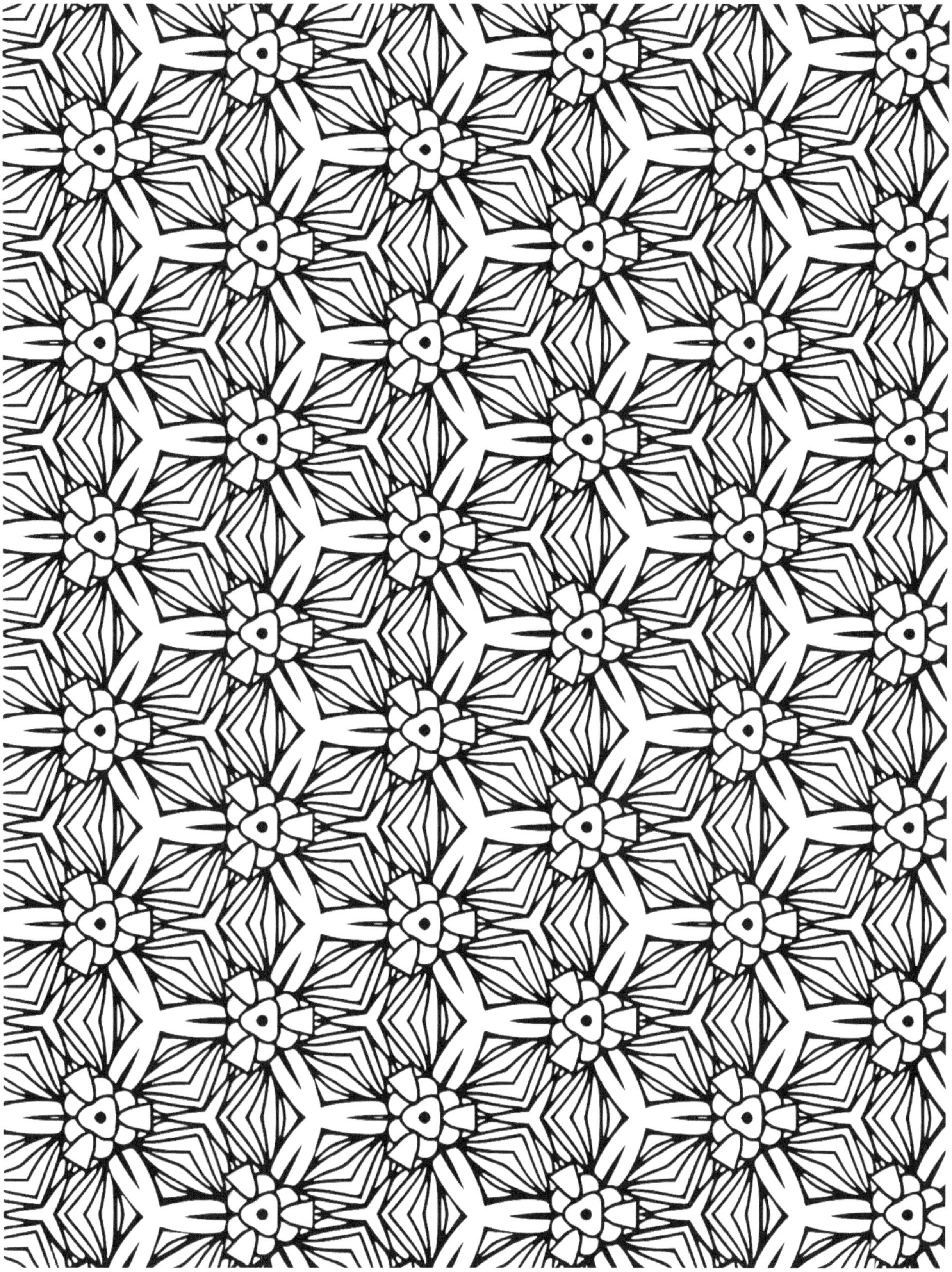

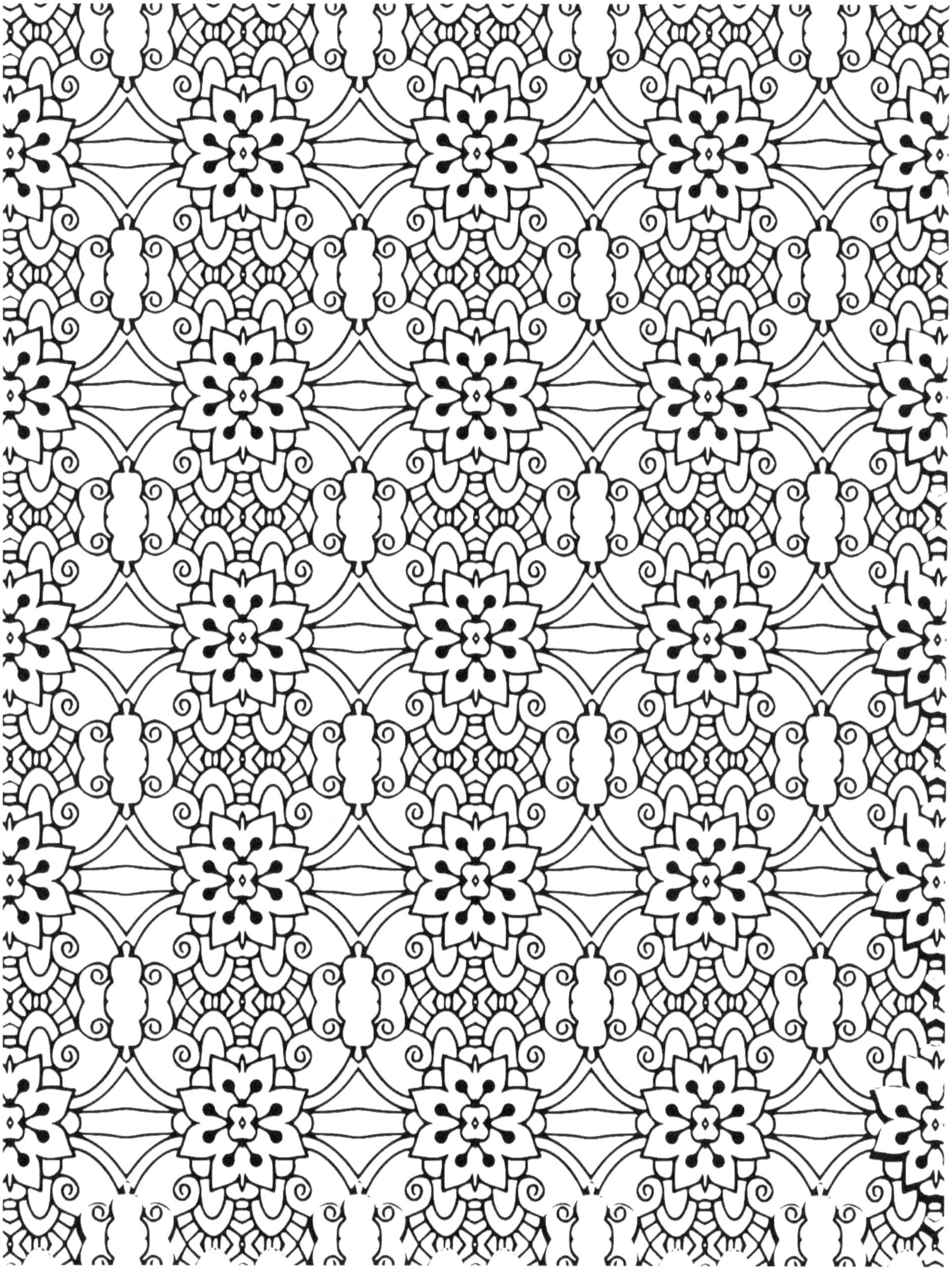

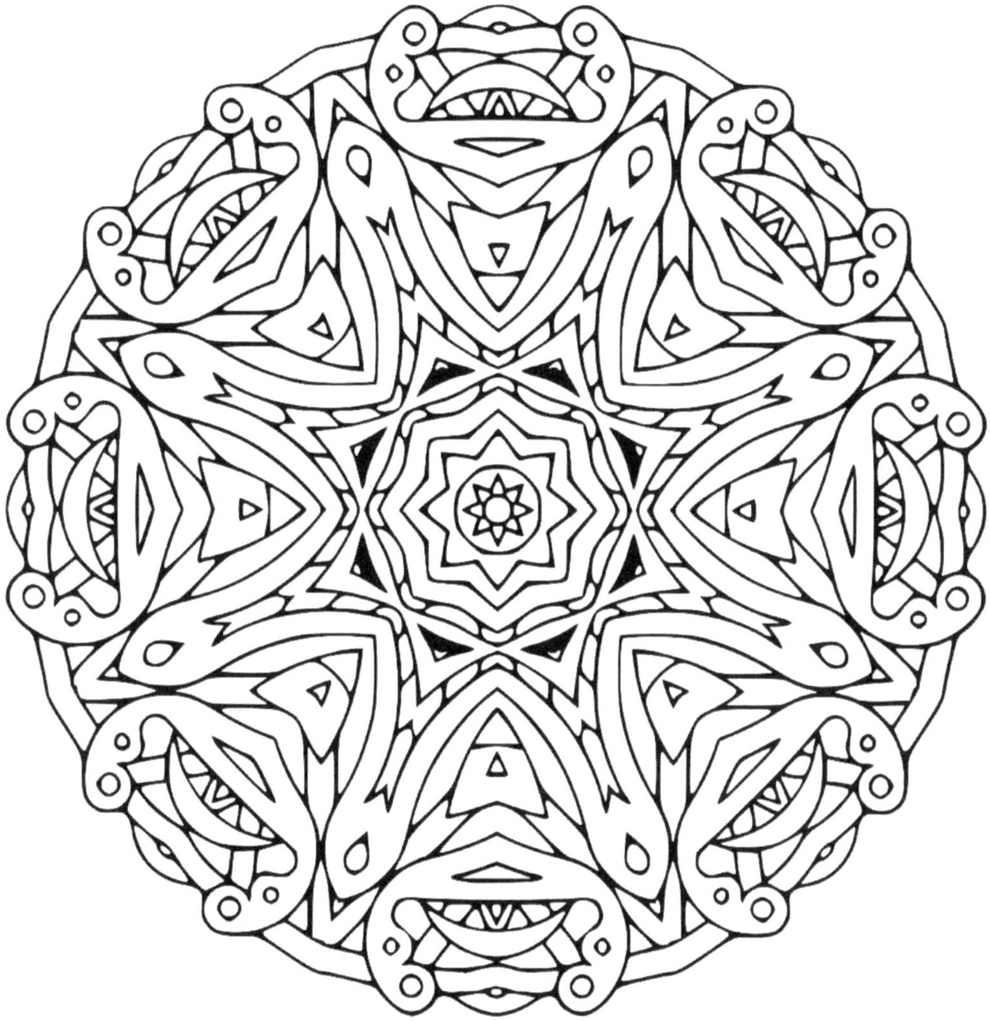

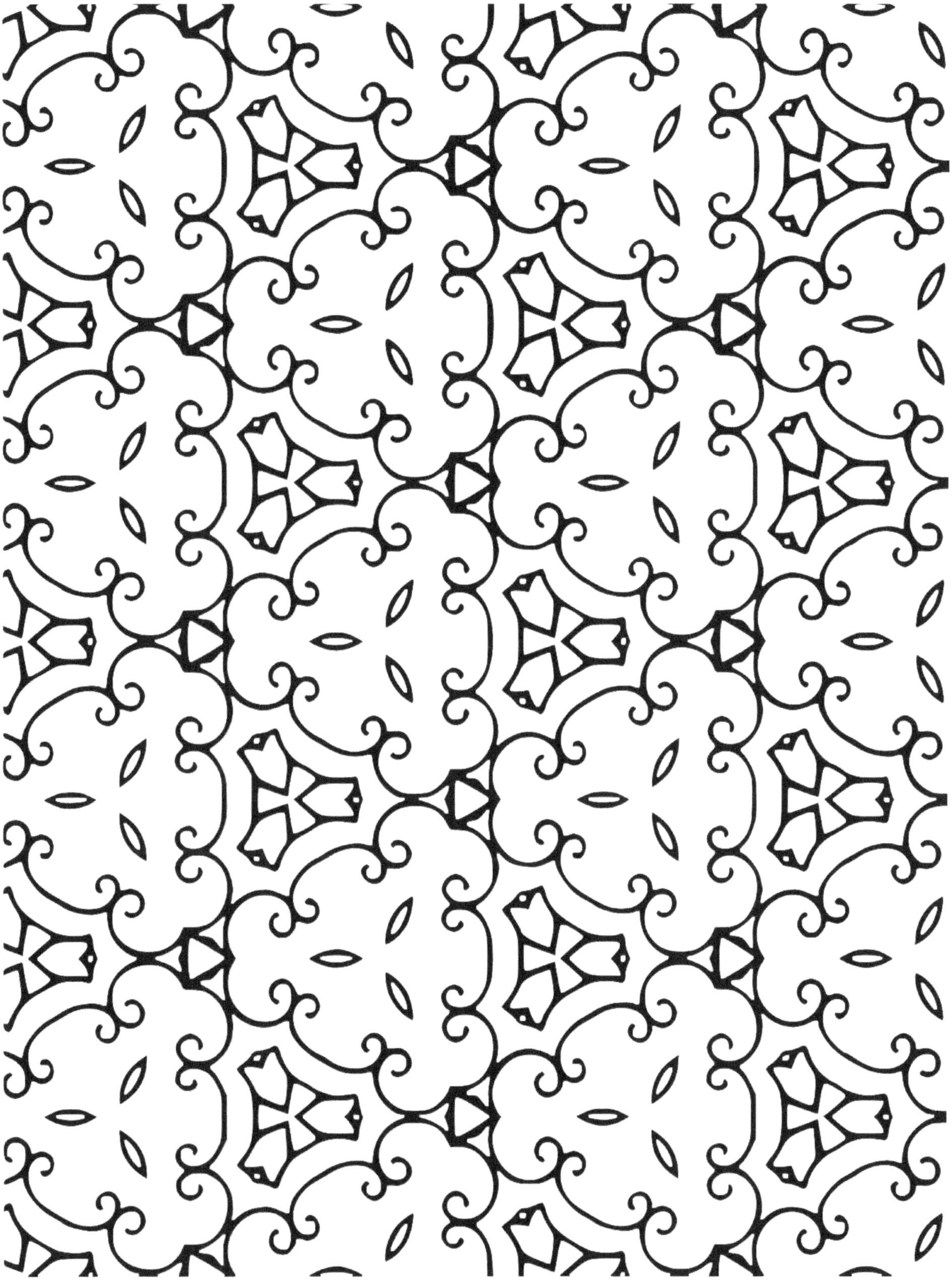

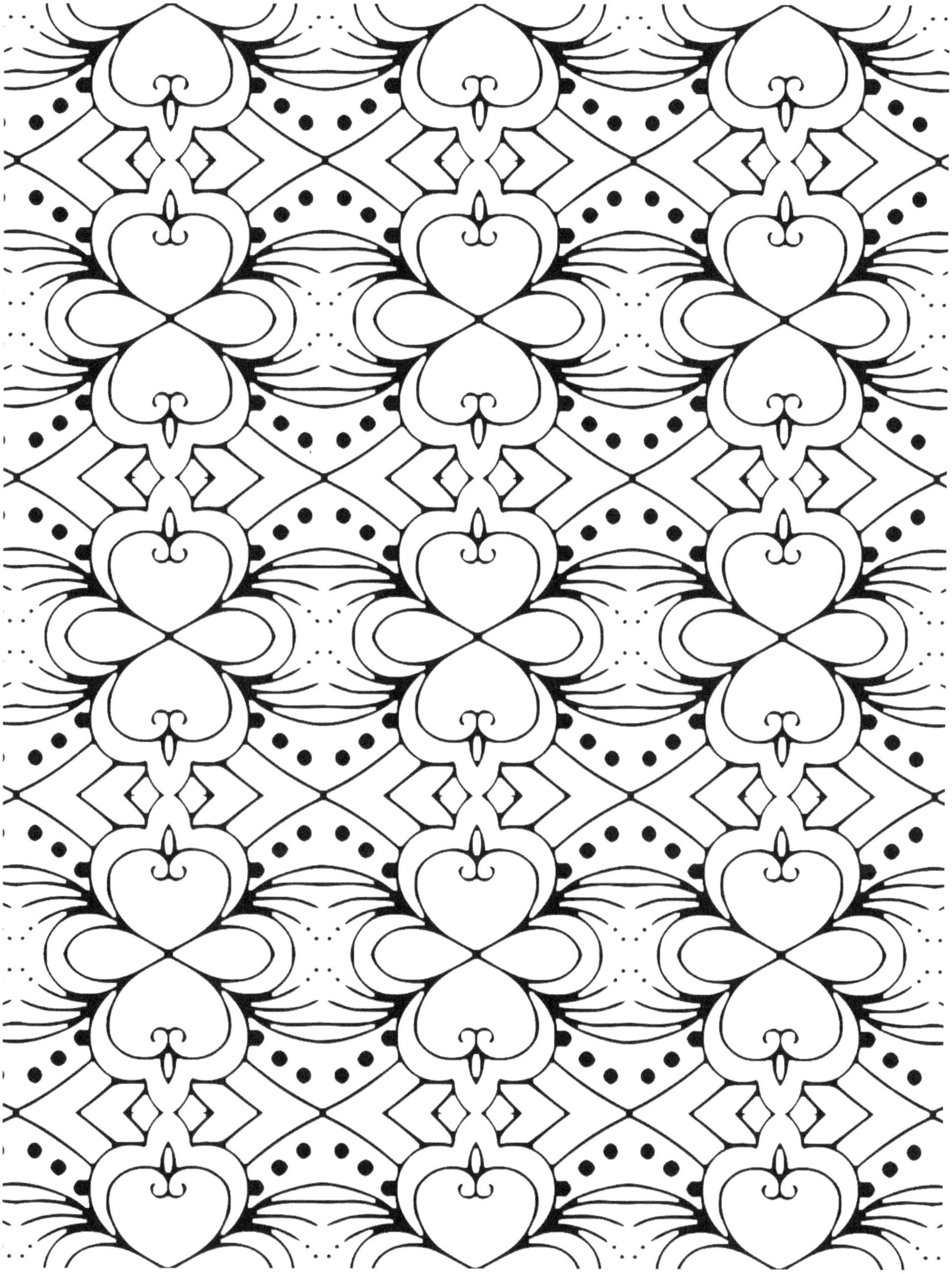

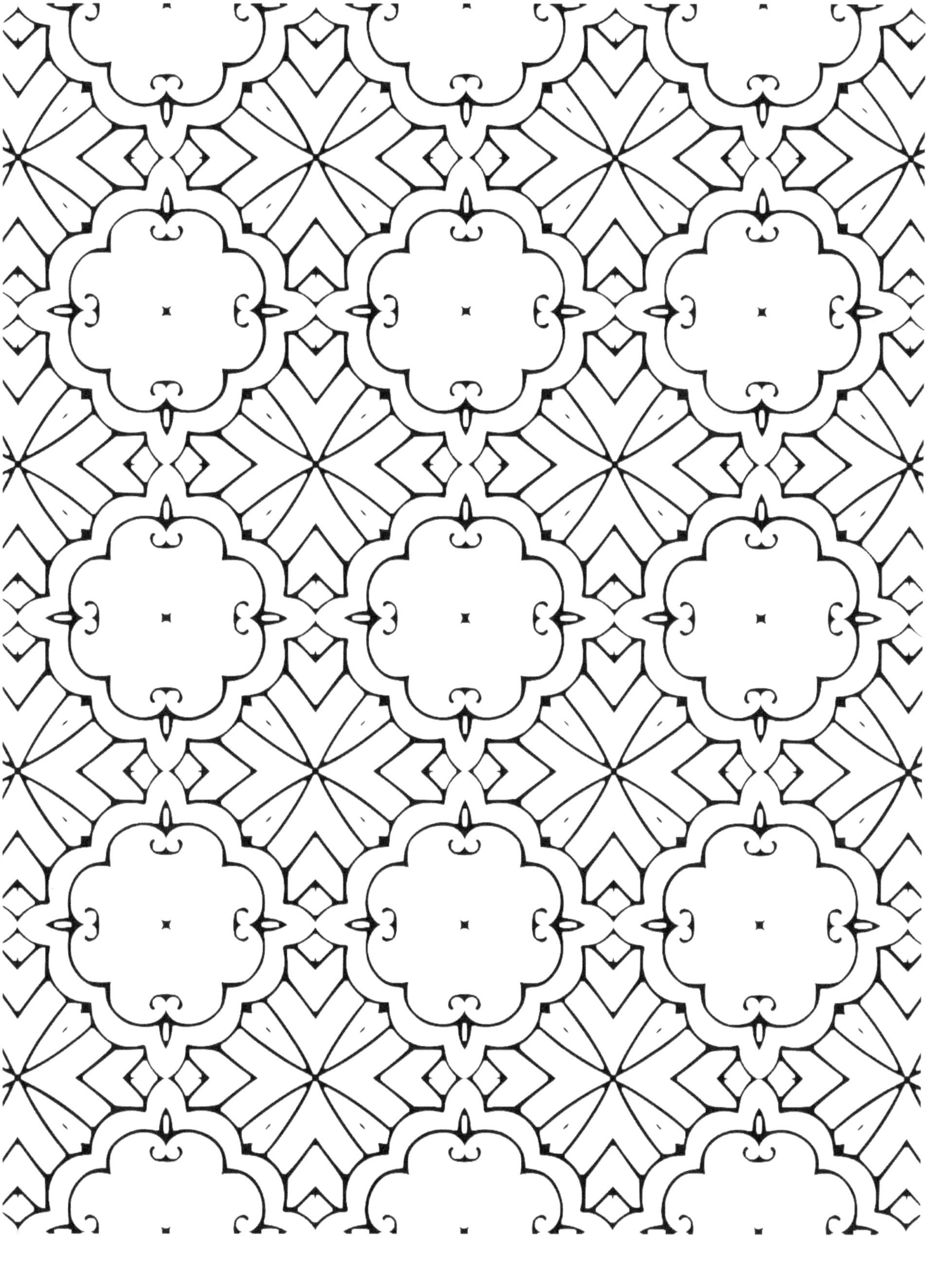

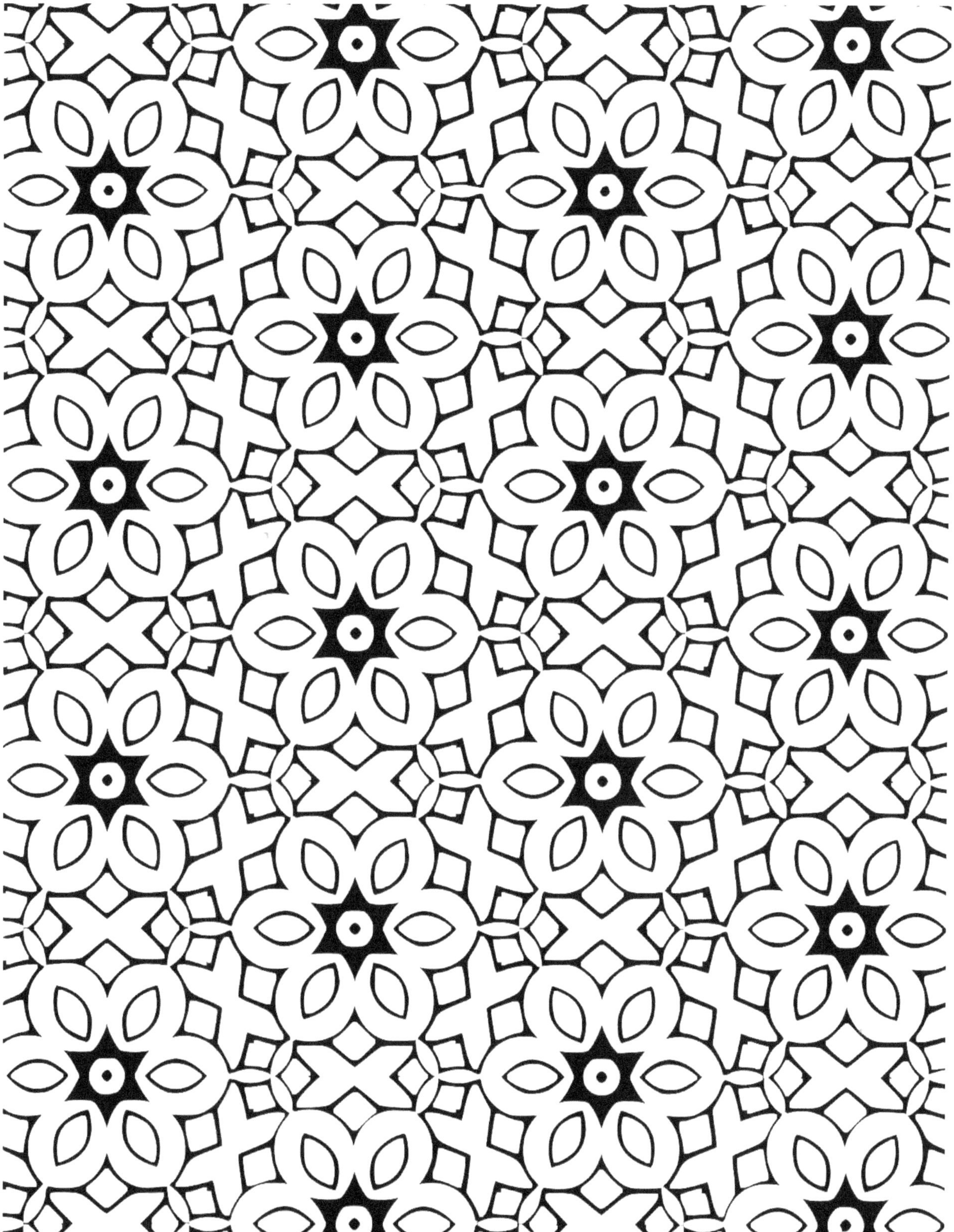

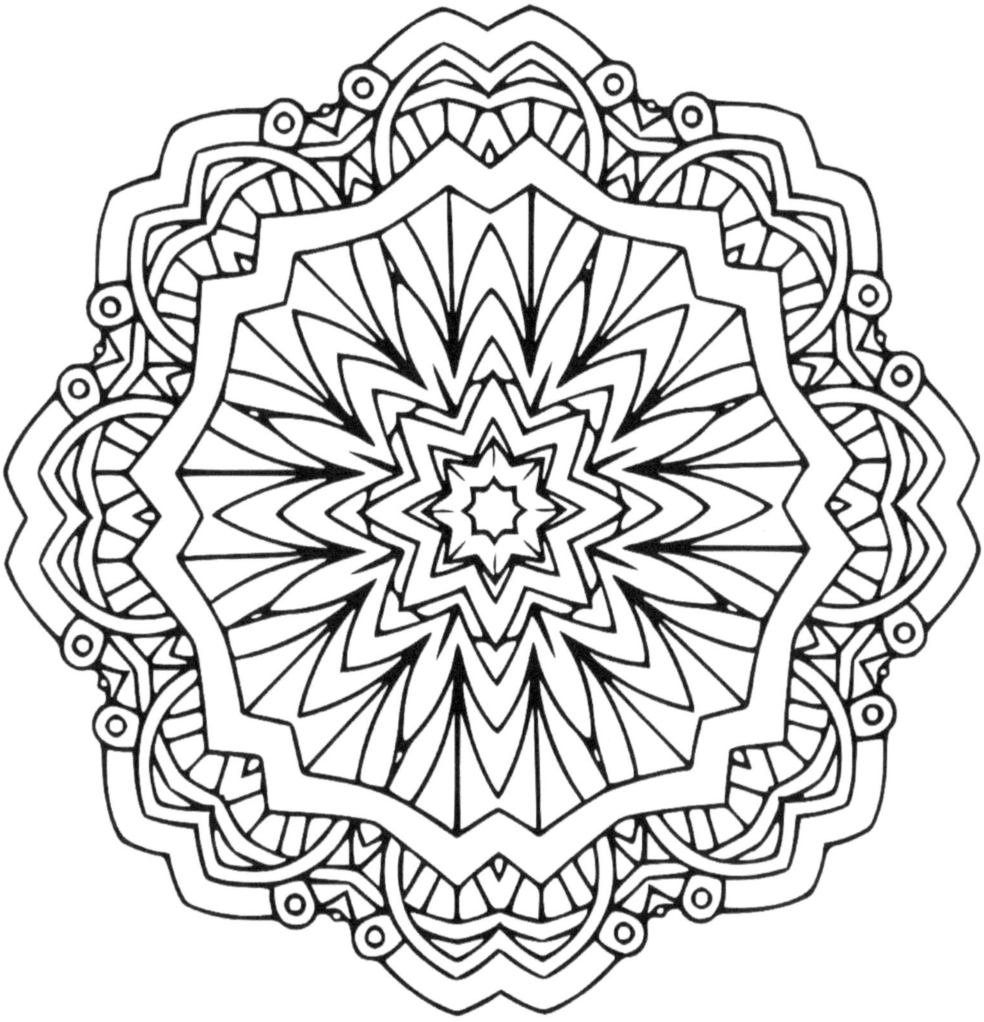

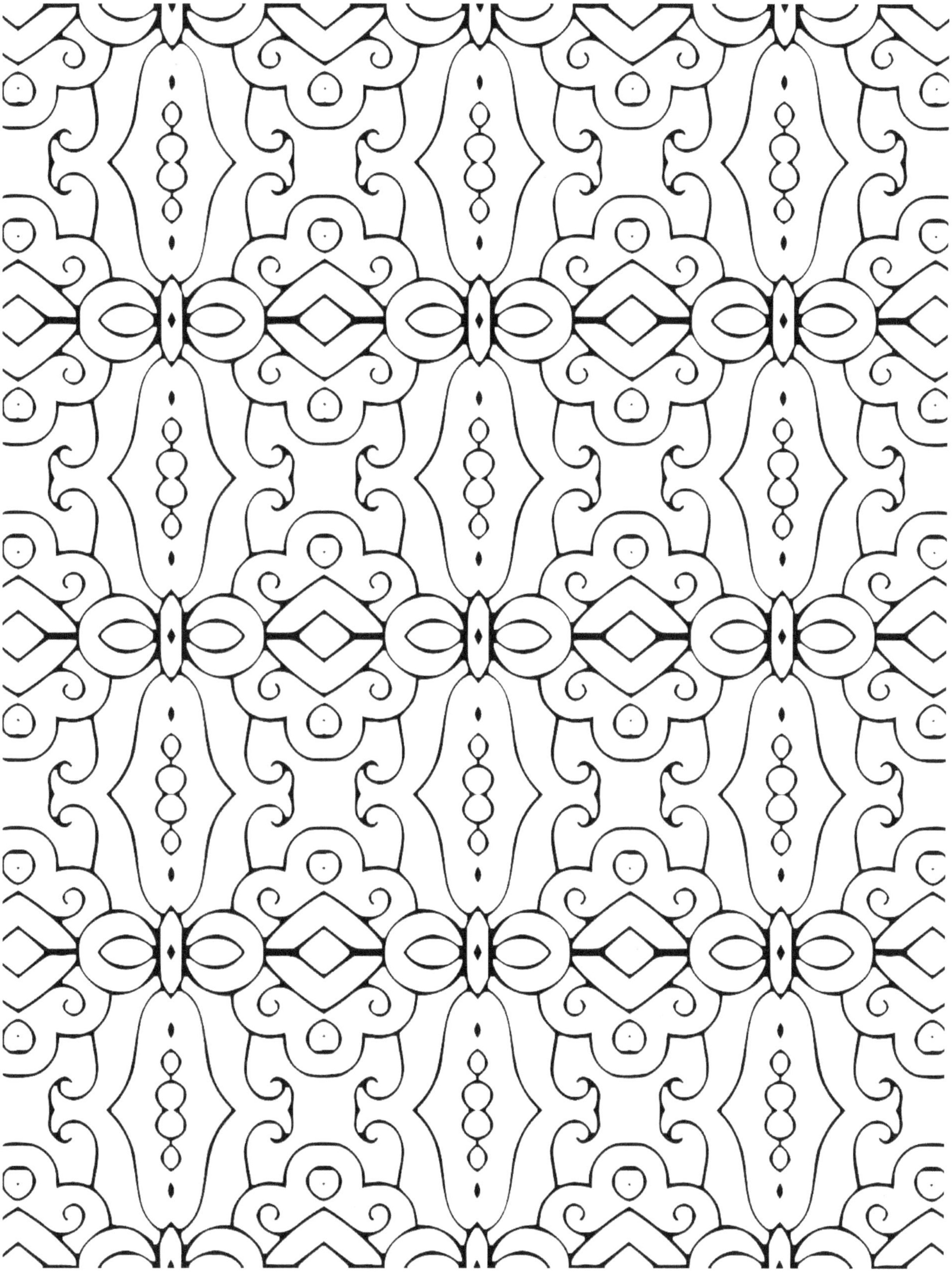

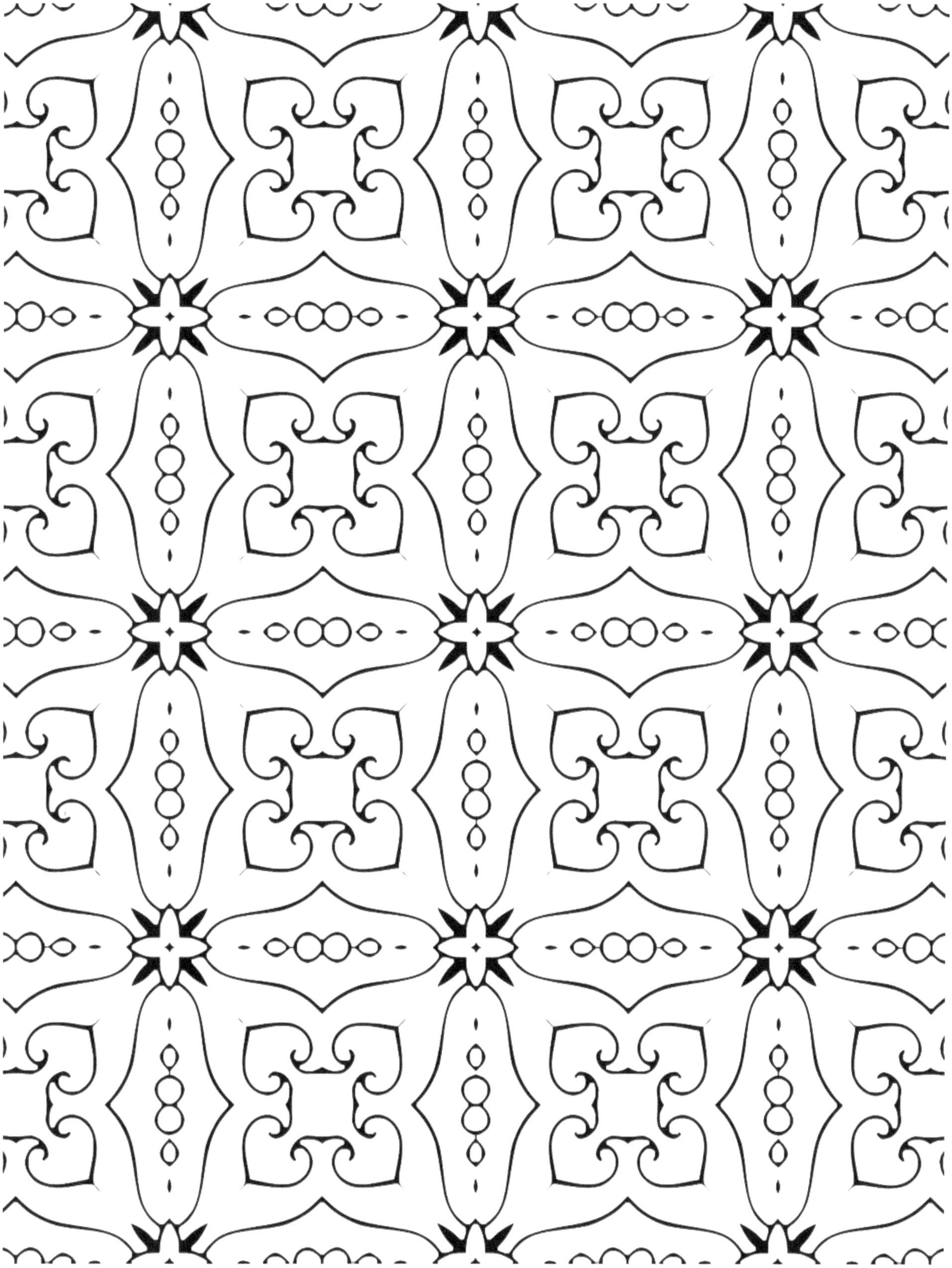

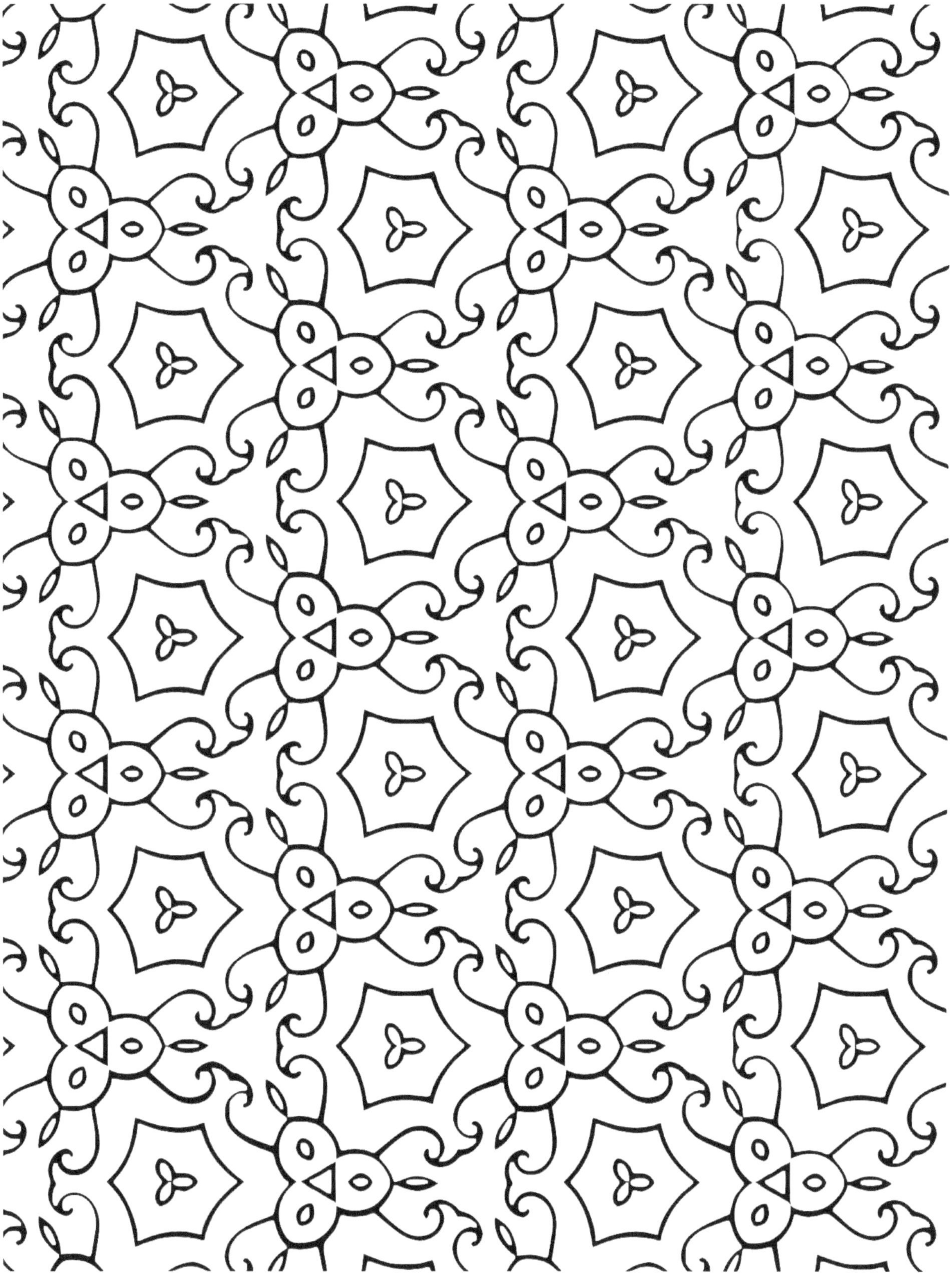

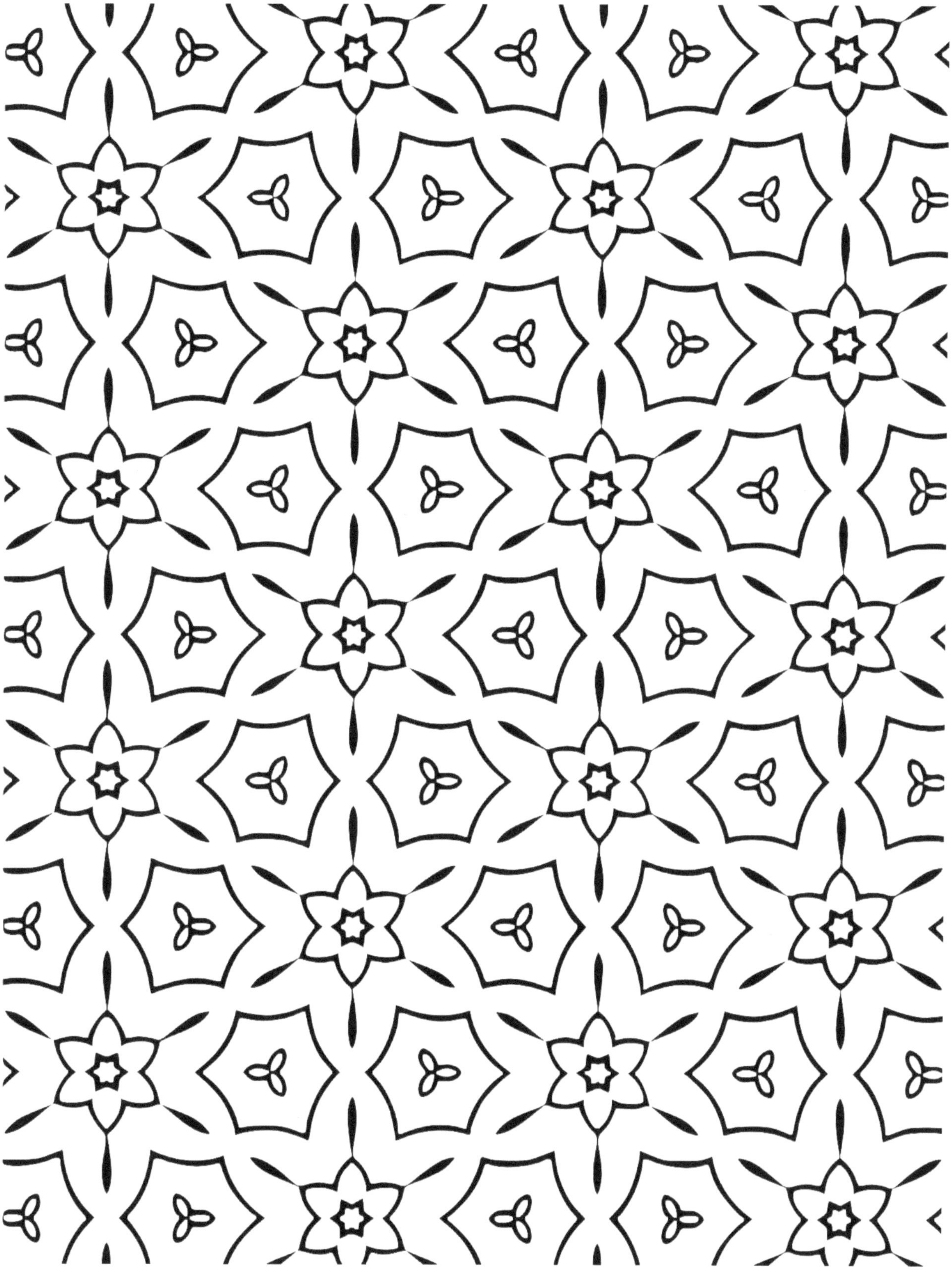

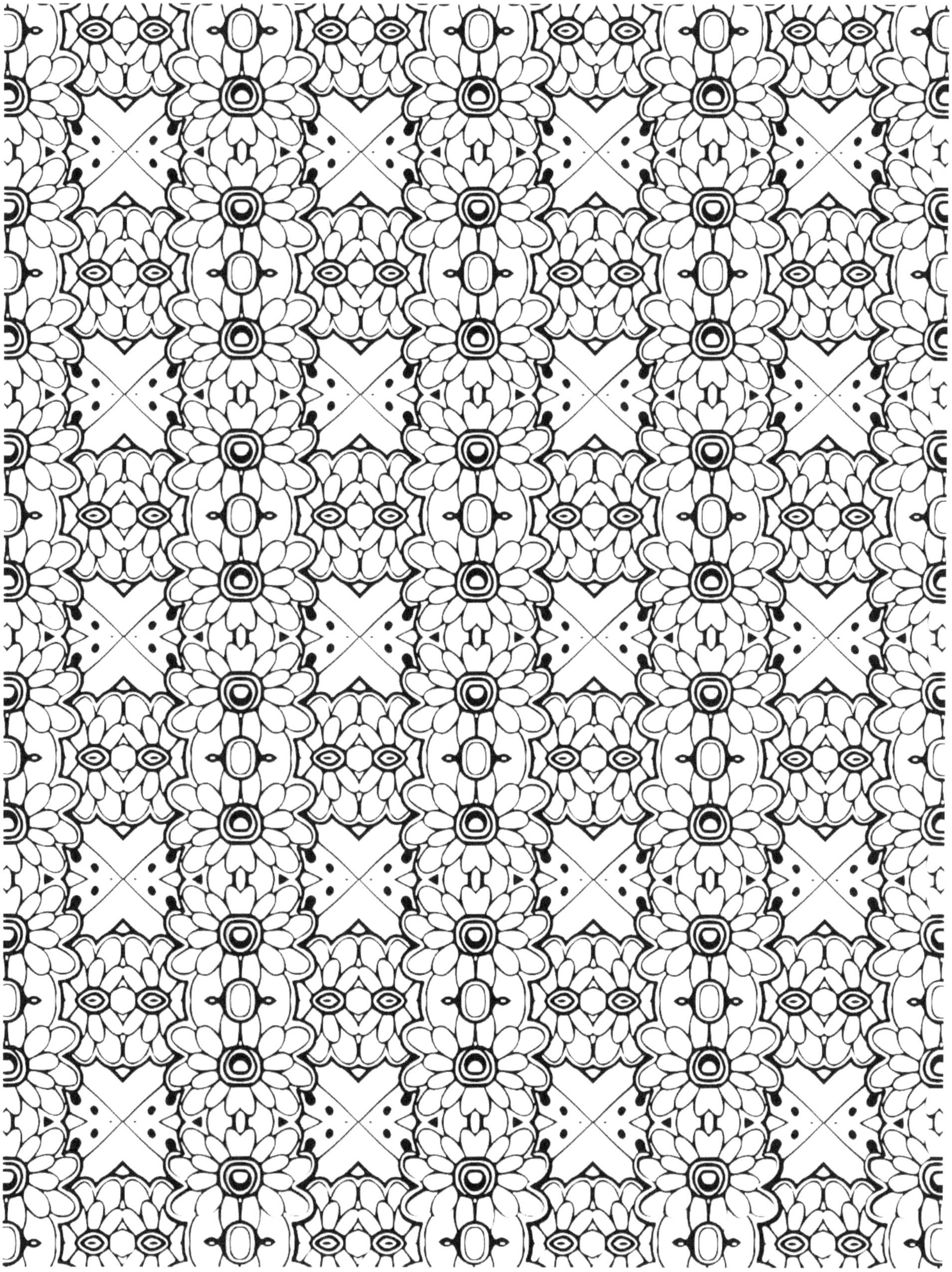

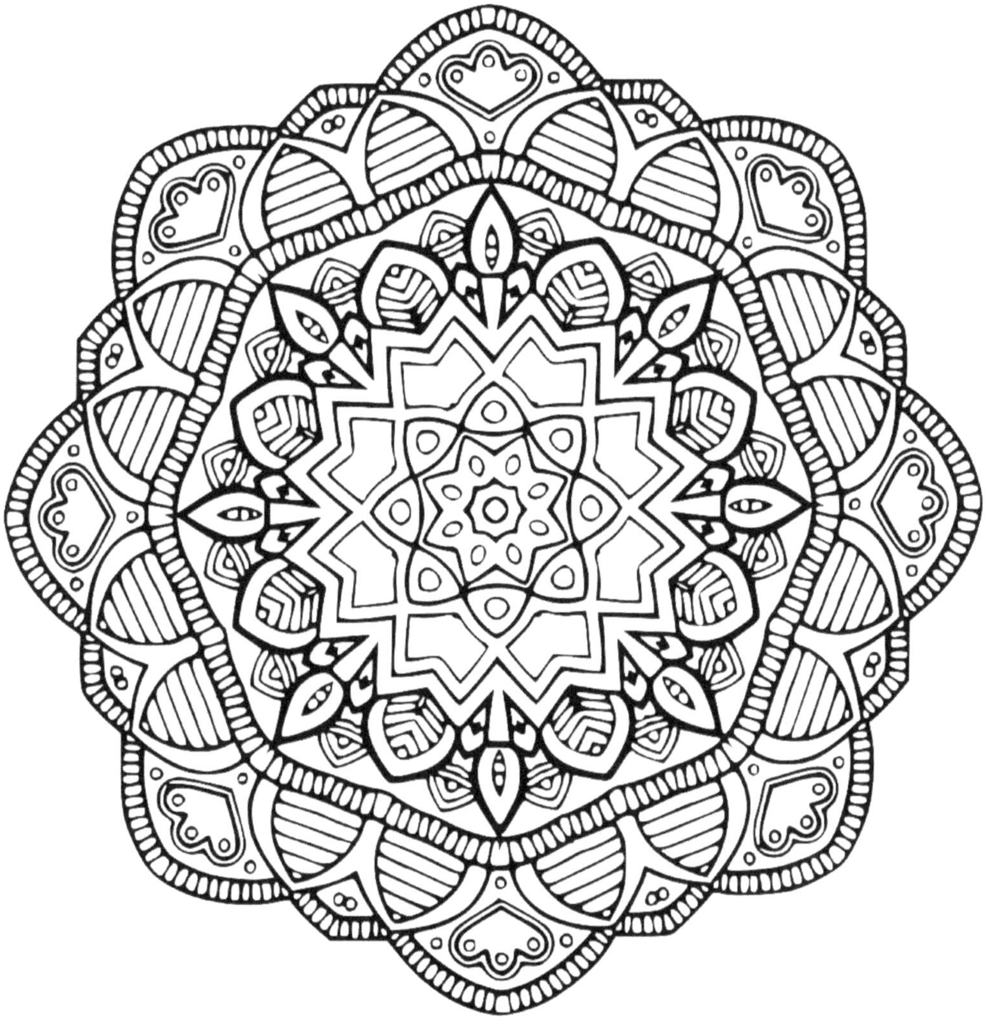

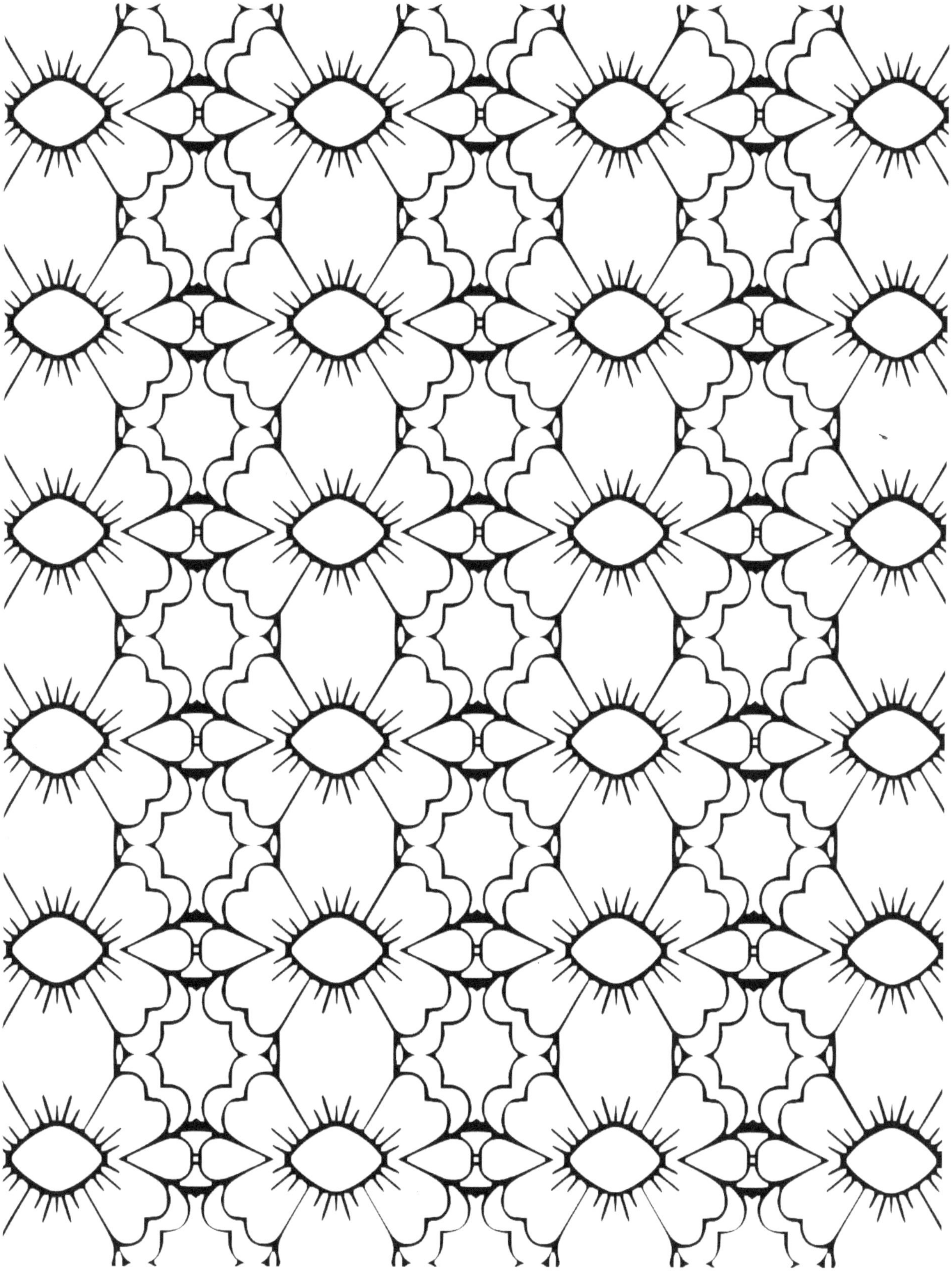

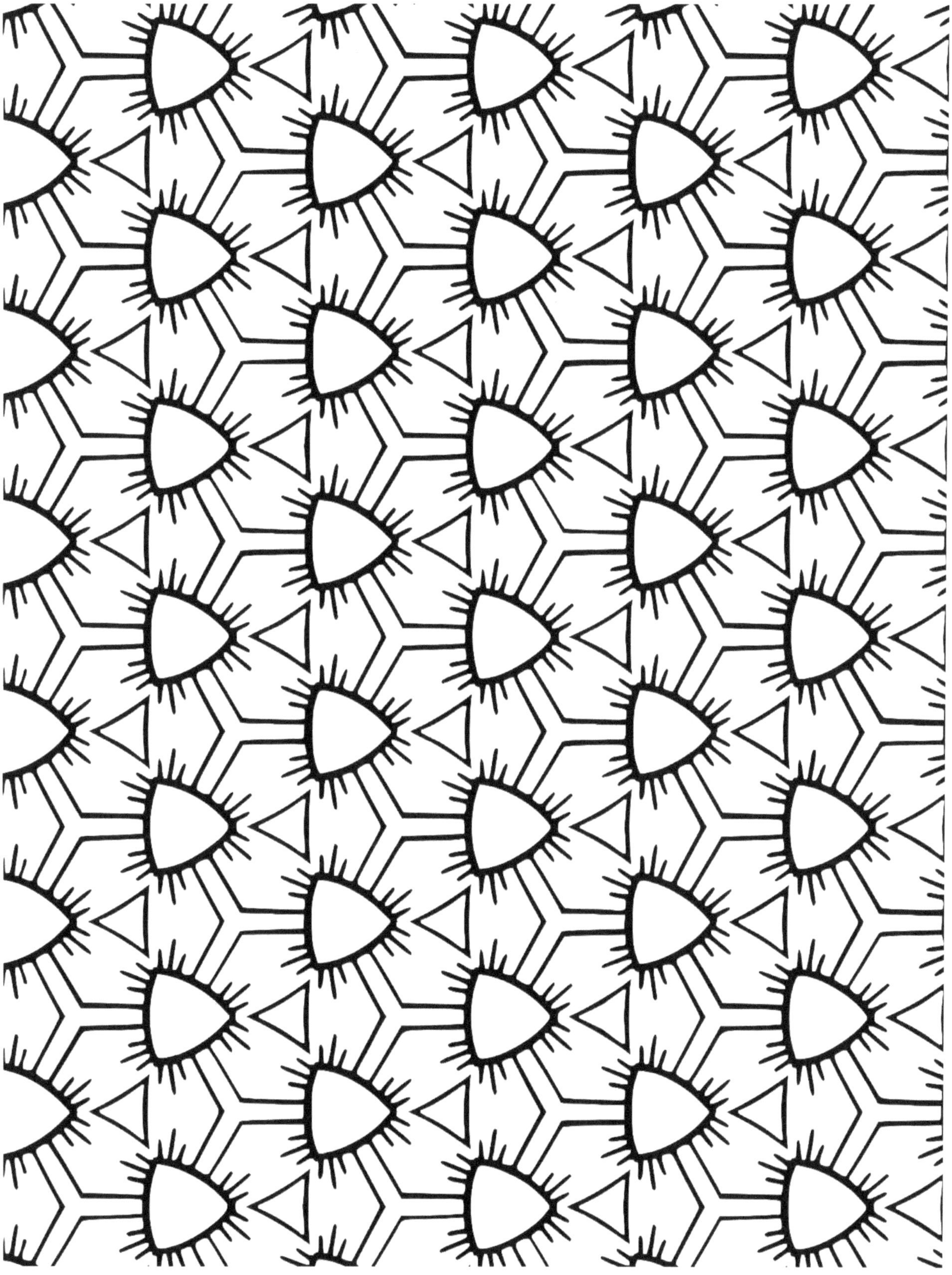

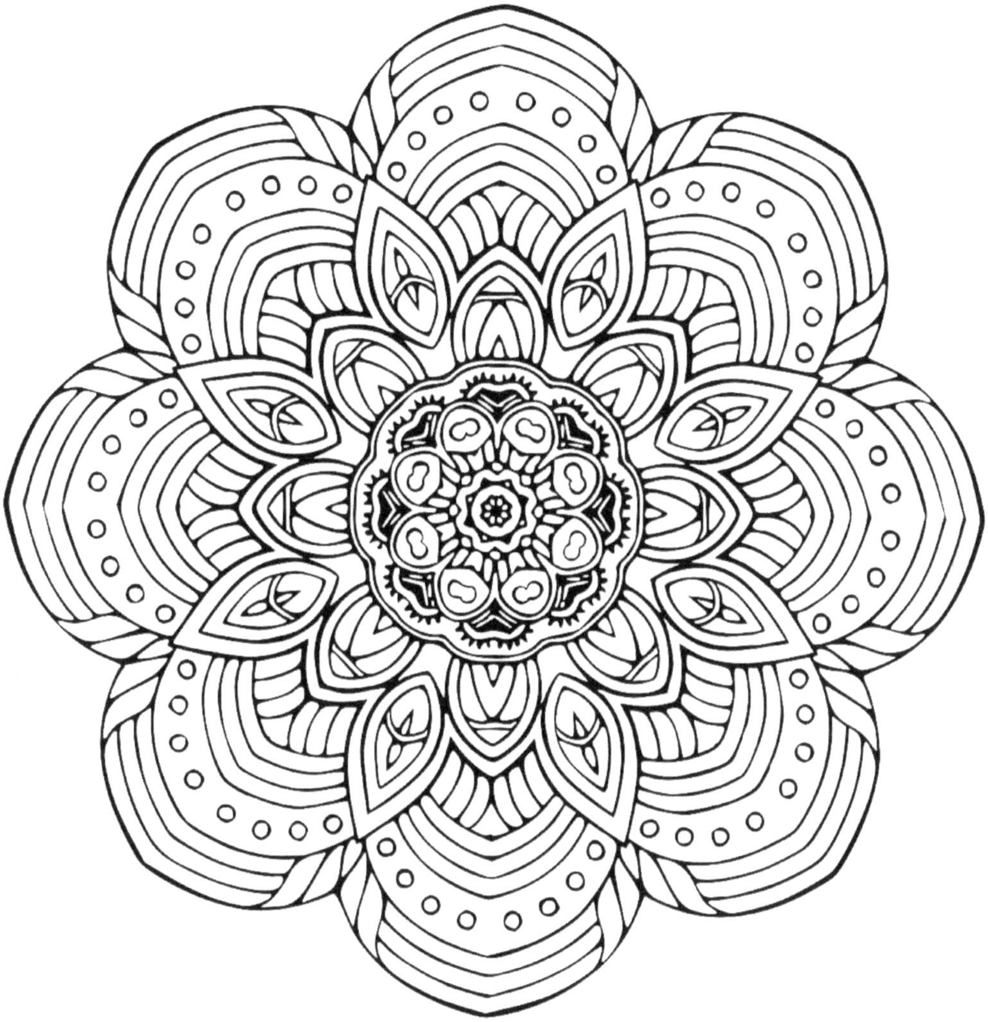

Thank you.

We hope you enjoyed our coloring book.

CVJ Publishing

www.ingramcontent.com/pod-product-compliance
Lightning Source LLC
Chambersburg PA
CBHW050849180526
45159CB00007B/2625
* 9 7 8 1 5 3 7 2 5 0 5 3 3 *